GUIDE TO GENEALOGICAL RECORDS IN THE NATIONAL ARCHIVES

By Meredith B. Colket, Jr.
and
Frank E. Bridgers

The National Archives
National Archives and Records Service
General Services Administration
Washington: 1964

NATIONAL ARCHIVES PUBLICATION NO. 64-8

Library of Congress Catalog Card No. A64-7048

For sale by the Superintendent of Documents, U.S. Government Printing Office
Washington, D.C., 20402 - Price 50 cents

FOREWORD

GSA through the National Archives and Records Service is responsible for administering the permanent noncurrent records of the Federal Government. These archival holdings, now amounting to over 900,000 cubic feet, date from the days of the Continental Congresses; they include the basic records of the three branches of our Government--Congress, the courts, and the executive departments and independent agencies. The Presidential Libraries--Hoover, Roosevelt, Truman, and Eisenhower--contain the papers of those Presidents and many of their associates in office. Among our holdings are many hallowed documents relating to great events of our Nation's history, preserved and venerated as symbols to stimulate a worthy patriotism in all of us. But most of the records are less dramatic, kept because of their continuing practical utility for the ordinary processes of government, for the protection of private rights, and for the research use of students and scholars.

To facilitate the use of the records and to describe their nature and content, our archivists prepare various kinds of finding aids. The present work is one such publication. We believe that it will prove valuable to anyone who wishes to use the records it describes.

BERNARD L. BOUTIN
Administrator of General Services

PREFACE

The records described in this guide are records of the Federal Government, created to satisfy legal requirements or to meet the administrative or other needs of the originating agencies. They were not originally made for genealogical purposes. The population census, for example, originated as a head count to determine representation in the House of Representatives; but this simple statistical purpose was expanded over the years, and in the process of collecting the basic data census schedules were completed, which show the names of all members of every household with their ages and other information that is genealogically valuable. Similarly the Federal Government, in administering its land and its military forces, has collected a wealth of other data useful for family history.

To use these records effectively a genealogist must know what kinds of information they contain and also, in most cases, how that information is arranged. For the arrangement of information in records limits the possibility of finding specific facts in them and determines what previous information is required to frame an answerable question. Most records are kept in the order that best served the needs of the creating agency: by name, date, number, place, organization, or a combination of these and other systems. If records are not arranged alphabetically and there are no indexes, certain identifying information in addition to the name of the person is usually needed to make an adequate search.

Most of the records here described, unless specific restrictions on their use are mentioned, may be freely used in the National Archives research rooms. Although the National Archives is not staffed to make extensive searches in the records, it will try to find a record about a person if it is given the essential facts necessary to search in the pertinent series. Photocopies of most of the documents can be furnished for a moderate fee. The National Archives does not construct family trees or trace lineage; nor does it maintain a list of persons who do research for a fee, but on request it will furnish the names and addresses of universities and other organizations in Metropolitan Washington that do provide the names of such persons.

Since 1940 the National Archives has been microfilming, as a form of publication, selected groups of records that have high research value. Under this program negative microfilm is retained by the National Archives and positive prints, known as microfilm publications, are made from these master negatives and sold at moderate cost. A *List of National Archives Microfilm Publications, 1961*, and a separate listing of *Federal Population Censuses, 1840-80*, are available upon request. Most series of records described in this guide that have been microfilmed are noted, but it should be remembered that other records are being microfilmed.

WAYNE C. GROVER
Archivist of the United States

CONTENTS

extant - still existing

I. POPULATION AND MORTALITY CENSUS SCHEDULES

The National Archives has census schedules of the Federal Government, 1790-1890. They include population census schedules, 1790-1890, and mortality census schedules, 1885. Information on their form, their contents, and aids to research in them follows. The National Archives has the schedules and research aids mentioned unless another location is given.

POPULATION CENSUS SCHEDULES

Information on the Form and Use of Schedules, by Census Year

The population census schedules in the National Archives comprise practically all the extant Federal population census schedules, 1790-1890. The schedules for some States and for some counties of other States, 1790-1820, and most schedules for 1890 are not extant. Most of the censuses were taken in decennial years; in addition there are 1857 schedules for Minnesota, 1864, 1866, 1867, and 1869 schedules for Arizona, and 1885 schedules for Colorado, Florida, Nebraska, and New Mexico. Information on the available form and the use of schedules for each census year is given below, followed by further specialized information for each State and Territory.

1790 Schedules

The records.--The 1790 schedules were created pursuant to an act of Congress approved March 1, 1790 (1 Stat. 101), which provided that the enumeration was to begin on the first Monday in August 1790 and to end within 9 months.

These schedules, which exist for most of the States in which the census was taken, are available normally only in printed form, in a single indexed volume for each State. The schedules therein are arranged by county and in some cases by minor subdivisions of counties. Other volumes based on local tax records have been printed in an effort to reconstruct missing schedules for some States.

Information in the records.--An entry shows the name of a head of family, the number of free white males of 16 years and upward in the household, the number of free white males under 16 years, the number of free white females, the number of all other free persons, and the number of slaves. The head of the family is included in the numerical statistics.

Research aids.--The county boundaries in 1790 and in 1900 of the Thirteen Original States and areas carved out of them--Maine, Vermont, Kentucky, Tennessee, and West Virginia--are shown on maps in Bureau of the Census, A Century of Population Growth, 1790-1900, p. 61-70 (Washington, 1909). These maps have been reprinted on a smaller scale in E. Kay Kirkham, Research in American Genealogy, p. 371 ff. (Salt Lake City, 1956).

The minor subdivisions of the counties for many of the States are given in Census Office, 1st Census, 1790, Return of the Whole Number of Persons Within the Several Districts of the United States, According to "An Act Providing for the Enumeration of the Inhabitants of the United States;" Passed March the First, One Thousand Seven Hundred and Ninety-One [i. e. 1790] (Philadelphia, 1793). The copy in the National Archives Library is a bound photocopy.

1800 Schedules

The records. --The 1800 schedules were created pursuant to an act of Congress approved February 28, 1800 (2 Stat. 11), which provided that the enumeration was to begin on the first Monday in August 1800 and to end within 9 months.

The extant schedules are available normally only as photostats in bound volumes or, for many of them, on microfilm. They are arranged by State or Territory, thereunder by county, and thereunder by minor subdivisions in some cases. Entries are arranged usually in the order of enumeration, rarely alphabetically to the first letter of the surname.

Information in the records. --An entry shows the name of a head of family; the numbers of free whites under 10 years of age, of 10 and under 16, of 16 and under 26, of 26 and under 45, and of 45 and upward in the household; the number of all other free persons except Indians not taxed; and the number of slaves. The head of the family is included in the numerical statistics.

Research aid. --The minor subdivisions of the counties for many of the States are given in Census Office, 2d Census, 1800, Return of the Whole Number of Persons Within the Several Districts of the United States . . . Second Census (Washington, 1801). The copy in the National Archives Library is a bound photocopy.

1810 Schedules

The records. --The 1810 schedules were created pursuant to an act of Congress approved March 26, 1810 (2 Stat. 564), which provided that the enumeration was to begin on the first Monday in August 1810 and to end within 9 months.

The extant schedules are available normally only as photostats in bound volumes or, for many of them, on microfilm. They are arranged by State or Territory, thereunder by county, and thereunder by minor subdivisions in some cases. Entries are arranged usually in order of enumeration.

Information in the records. --An entry shows the name of a head of family; the numbers of free white males under 10 years of age, of 10 and under 16, of 16 and under 45, and of 45 and upward in the household; the numbers of free white females under 10 years of age, of 10 and under 16, of 16 and under 26, of 26 and under 45, and of 45 and upward; the number of all other free persons except Indians not taxed; and the number of slaves. The head of the family is included in the numerical statistics.

Research aid.--For indentification of the minor subdivisions of the counties, see Census Office, 3d Census, 1810, Aggregate Amount of Each

Description of Persons Within the United States of America, and the Territories Thereof, Agreeably To Actual Enumeration Made According to Law, in the Year 1810 (Washington, 1811).

1820 Schedules

The records.--The 1820 schedules were created pursuant to an act of Congress approved March 14, 1820 (3 Stat. 548), which provided that the enumeration was to begin on the first Monday in August 1820 and to end within 6 months.

The extant schedules are available normally only as photostats in bound volumes or for many of them, on microfilm. They are arranged by State or Territory, thereunder by county, and thereunder by minor subdivisions in some cases. Entries are usually arranged in the order of enumeration.

Information in the records.--An entry shows the name of a head family; the numbers of free white males under 10 years of age, of 10 and under 16, between 16 and 18, of 16 and under 26, of 26 and under 45, of 45 and upward in the household; the numbers of free white females under 10 years of age, of 10 and under 16, of 16 and under 26, of 26 and under 45, of 45 and upward; the number of foreigners not naturalized; the number of persons engaged in agriculture, in commerce, and in manufactures; the numbers of free colored persons and of slaves, by sex and various age groups; and the number of all other persons except Indians not taxed. The head of the family is included in the numerical statistics.

Research aids.--For the minor subdivisions of the counties see Census Office, 4th Census, 1820, Census for 1820 (Washington, 1821).

1830 Schedules

The records.--The 1830 schedules were created pursuant to an act of Congress approved March 23, 1830 (4 Stat. 383), which provided that the enumeration was to begin on June 1, 1830, and to end within 6 months.

These schedules are on printed forms uniform in size. Each entry is on two facing pages. The left-hand pages contain chiefly family data, the right-hand pages slave data. The schedules are available as photostats in bound volumes and as microfilm copies. They are arranged by State or Territory, thereunder by county, and thereunder by minor subdivisions in some cases.

Information in the records.--An entry shows the name of a head of family; the numbers of free white persons under 5 years of age, of 5 and under 10, of 10 and under 15, of 15 and under 20, of 20 and under 30, of 30 and under 40, of 40 and under 50, of 50 and under 60, of 60 and under 70, of 70 and under 80, of 80 and under 90, of 90 and under 100, of 100 and upward in the household; the numbers of free white females in each of the same age groups; the numbers of slaves and of free colored persons by sex and various age groups; and the number of aliens. The head of the family is included in the numerical statistics.

Research aids. In a number of instances the schedules relating to a county are in more than one volume of the schedules. When searches are to be made in the schedules for such a county and the name of the township within the county is known, the identification of the appropriate volume can be made by consulting the one-volume typed checklist of the 1830 population census schedules. This shows the names of the counties covered by each volume of the schedules; and, if the schedules for a county are in more than one volume, the names of the townships.

For minor subdivisions of the counties see Census Office, 5th Census, 1830, Fifth Census; or, Enumeration of the Inhabitants of the United States, as Corrected at the Department of State, 1830 (Washington, 1832). The copy in the National Archives is bound in a volume with other publications relating to the 1830 census and begins on a page numbered 199 in pencil.

1840 Schedules

The records.--The 1840 schedules were created pursuant to an act of Congress approved March 3, 1839 (5 Stat. 331), which provided that the enumeration was to begin June 1, 1840, and to end within 10 months.

These schedules are on printed forms uniform in size. Each entry is on two facing pages. The left-hand page contains chiefly family data; the right-hand page, chiefly slave, employment, and pension data. The schedules are available in bound volumes and on microfilm. They are arranged by State or Territory, thereunder by county, and thereunder by minor subdivision in most cases. The entries are usually arranged in order of enumeration.

Information in the records.--An entry shows the name of a head of family; the numbers of free white persons under 5 years of age, of 5 and under 10, of 10 and under 15, of 15 and under 20, of 20 and under 30, of 30 and under 40, of 40 and under 50, of 50 and under 60, of 60 and under 70, of 70 and under 80, of 80 and under 90, of 90 and under 100, of 100 and upward in the household; the numbers of free white females in each of the same age groups; the numbers of slaves and of free colored persons by sex and various age groups; the numbers of persons in each family engaged in various classes of occupations; and the names and ages of any military pensioners.

Research aids.--An outline map prepared by the Department of Agriculture shows the name and location of each county in the United States in 1840. The copy in the National Archives is in a binder with other outline maps.

The names and ages of the pensioners listed in the schedules have been printed in Department of State, A Census of Pensioners for Revolutionary or Military Services (Washington, 1841). Some pensioners listed in this volume are not Federal pensioners, and it is therefore presumed that they are State pensioners inadvertently included in the list. A carbon copy and a positive microfilm copy of a two-volume typescript index to the volume is available in the National Archives; the ribbon copy and a negative microfilm copy are in the custody of the Utah Genealogical Society.

The minor subdivisions of the counties are given in Census Office, 6th Census, 1840, Sixth Census or Enumeration of the Inhabitants of the United States, as Corrected at the Department of State in 1840 (Washington 1841).

1850 Schedules

The records.--The 1850 schedules were created pursuant to an act of Congress approved May 23, 1850 (9 Stat. 428), which provided that the census was to begin June 1, 1850.

These schedules on printed forms are available in bound volumes and on microfilm. They are divided into schedules for the free inhabitants and, for the appropriate States or Territories, schedules for the slave inhabitants. Schedules in each part are arranged by name of State or Territory, thereunder by name of county, and thereunder by name of minor subdivision.

Information in the records.--For each free person in a household an entry shows the name and postal address; age, sex, and color (white, black, or mulatto); occupation if over 15 years of age; the value of real estate owned; the State, Territory, or country of birth; and whether or not he was married within the year.

For each slave an entry shows the name of the slaveowner; the age, sex, and color (but not the name) of the slave; and whether or not he was a fugitive from the State. There is also a column for the number of slaves manumitted by each slaveowner.

Research aids.--A volume index, contained in two looseleaf binders, shows for each State or Territory the name of the county, the name of the minor subdivision, and the volume number and inclusive page numbers of the schedules. If the schedules for a county are in more than one volume and the searcher knows the name of the minor subdivision of the schedules in which he is interested, he can identify the volume number from the appropriate index.

For a printed list of minor subdivisions see "Population by Subdivisions of Counties" in Census Office, 7th Census, 1850, The Seventh Census of the United States: 1850, Embracing a Statistical View of Each of the States and Territories, Arranged by Counties, Towns, etc. (Washington, 1853).

An outline map prepared by the Department of Agriculture shows the name and location of each county in the United States in 1850. The copy in the National Archives is in a binder with other outline maps.

1857 Schedules for Minnesota Territory

The records.--The 1857 schedules for Minnesota Territory were created pursuant to section 4 of an act of Congress approved February 26, 1857 (11 Stat. 167), to enable Minnesota Territory to become a State. The schedules are on printed forms in five volumes. They are arranged alphabetically by name of county, thereunder by minor subdivision. The enumeration was taken as of September 21, 1857.

Information in the records.--For each inhabitant of a household an entry shows the name; his age, sex, and color, the State, Territory, or country of birth; if a voter, whether native or naturalized; and his occupation.

1860 Schedules

The records.--The 1860 schedules were created pursuant to an act of Congress approved May 23, 1850 (9 Stat. 428), which provided that the census was to begin June 1.

These schedules on printed forms are available in bound volumes and on microfilm. They are divided into schedules for the free inhabitants and, for the appropriate States, schedules for the slave inhabitants. Schedules in each part are arranged by name of State or Territory, thereunder by name of county, and thereunder by name of minor subdivision.

Information in the records.--For each free person in a household an entry shows the name and postal address; age, sex, and color (white, black, or mulatto); occupation if over 15 years of age; the value of his real estate; the value of his personal estate; the name of the State, Territory, or country of birth; and whether or not he was married within the year.

For each slave an entry shows the name of the slaveowner; the age, sex, and color (but not the name) of the slave; and whether or not he was a fugitive from the State. There is also a column for the number of slaves manumitted by the slaveowner.

Research aids.--The schedules relating to some counties are in more than one volume. If a search is made in the schedules of such a county and the name of the local subdivision is known, the searcher should see a typed checklist entitled "State and Counties by Volumes . . . 1860." This shows the names of the counties covered by each volume of the schedules; and, if the schedules for a county are in more than one volume, the names of the townships in each volume.

The names of the cities, towns, and other minor subdivisions of the counties in 1860 are listed under the name of each State and Territory in Census Office, 8th Census, 1860, Population of the United States in 1860; Compiled from the Original Returns of the Eighth Census (Washington, 1864).

An outline map prepared by the Department of Agriculture shows the name and location of each county in the United States in 1860. The copy in the National Archives is in a binder with other outline maps.

1864 Schedules for Arizona

The records.--The National Archives has photostats in two volumes and typed and mimeographed copies of the Arizona schedules of 1864. The originals, in the custody of the Secretary of State, Phoenix, were created in accordance with a proclamation of December 29, 1863, by the Territorial Governor. The schedules are arranged by judicial district (of which there were three) and thereunder by name of minor subdivision.

Information in the records.--For each person in a household an entry shows the name, age, sex, and marital status; the number of years and months of residence; where appropriate, brief naturalization data; the place of residence of the family of a married person enumerated; occupation; and the value of his real and personal estate.

1866, 1867, and 1869 Schedules for Arizona

The records.--Photostats of Arizona schedules of 1866, 1867, and 1869, in one volume, are available. The schedules are arranged by name of county. The following list identifies by census year the names of the counties for which schedules are available:

1866: Pahute, Mohave, Pima, Yuma, and Yavapai
1867: Mohave, Pima, and Yuma
1869: Yavapai

Information in the records.--For each person in a household an entry shows the name; the place of residence; whether head of family; and whether over 21, over 10 and under 21, or under 10.

1870 Schedules

The records.--The 1870 schedules were created pursuant to an act of Congress approved May 23, 1850 (9 Stat. 428), which provided in part that the enumeration was to begin June 1. Schedules on printed forms in bound volumes are arranged by name of State or Territory, thereunder by name of county, and thereunder by minor subdivision. The schedules are also available on microfilm.

Information in the records.--For each person in a household an entry shows the name and postal address; age (if under 1, the number of months), sex, and color (white, black, mulatto, Chinese, Indian); occupation; the value of his real estate; the value of his personal estate; the name of the State, Territory, or country of birth; whether his father was of foreign birth; whether his mother was of foreign birth; the month of birth if born within the year; the month of marriage if married within the year; and whether a male citizen 21 years or more.

Research aids.--For information about minor subdivisions in 1870, see "Population of Civil Divisions Less than Counties" in Census Office, 9th Census, 1870, *The Statistics of the Population of the United States. . . Compiled from the Original Returns of the Ninth Census (June 1, 1870)*, p. 77-296 (Washington, 1872).

An outline map prepared by the Department of Agriculture shows the name and location of each county in the United States in 1870. The copy in the National Archives is in a binder with other outline maps.

1880 Schedules

The records.--The 1880 schedules were created pursuant to an act of Congress approved March 3, 1879 (20 Stat. 473). This act provided that the enumeration was to begin on the first Monday in June 1880.

The schedules are available in the National Archives only in microfilm form. The microfilm was made from the fragile original schedules, which in 1956 were transferred from the National Archives to non-Federal depositories. The National Archives has a list showing where the schedules for each State were sent.

The schedules are arranged by name of State or Territory, thereunder by name of county, and thereunder by name of minor subdivision. The areas within a State were divided into supervisor's districts and thereunder into enumeration districts.

Information in the records.--For each person in a household an entry shows the name of the street and house number, if any; the name of the person and his postal address; color, sex, and age (if under 1, number of months); if born within the census year, the month of birth; relationship to the head of the family; whether single, married, widowed, or divorced; whether married during the census year; occupation; and the name of the State, Territory, or country of his birth, of his father's birth, and of his mother's birth.

Research aids.--The boundaries of the enumeration districts for many States and Territories are described on printed forms bound in four volumes entitled "Tenth Census 1880 Description of Enumeration Districts" and in a typed transcript of such forms in a seven-volume set. Some variations as to completeness exist between the two sets. They are particularly useful for searches in urban areas because exact street boundaries are given.

747-596 O - 64 - 2

The National Archives has volumes for the following States and Territories: Dakota (part), Delaware (part), District of Columbia, Florida, Georgia, Idaho, Illinois, Indiana, Iowa, Kansas, Kentucky, Louisiana, Maine, Maryland, Massachusetts, Michigan, Minnesota, Mississippi, Missouri, Nebraska, Nevada, New Hampshire, New Jersey, New Mexico, New York, North Carolina, Rhode Island, South Carolina, Tennessee, Texas, Utah, Vermont, Virginia, Washington, West Virginia, and Wyoming.

For information about minor subdivisions in 1880, including a comparison with those of 1870, see "Population of Civil Divisions Less Than Counties" in Census Office, 10th Census, 1880, Statistics of the Population of the United States at the Tenth Census, p. 93-375 (Washington, 1883).

The National Archives has an outline map prepared by the Department of Agriculture showing the name and location of each county in 1880.

The National Archives has a microfilm copy of a card index to those entries on the 1880 schedules that relate to households containing a child aged 10 or under. The cards contain the names, ages, and birthplaces of all members of such households, and there is a separate cross-reference card for each child aged 10 or under whose surname is different from that of the head of the household in which he is listed. The cards are arranged by State and thereunder by the Soundex system; that is, alphabetically by the first letter of the surname, thereunder by the sound of the surname, and thereunder alphabetically by given name of the head of the household.

1885 Schedules for Colorado, Florida, Nebraska, and New Mexico

The records.--The 1885 schedules were created pursuant to section 22 of an act of Congress approved March 3, 1879 (20 Stat. 480). The act provided in part that the States or Territories that elected to take an 1885 census modeled after that of 1880 would be partially reimbursed by the Federal Government. The States or Territories that took advantage of this provision of the act were Colorado, Dakota, Florida, Nebraska, and New Mexico. The schedules for all except Dakota are in the National Archives, unbound; those for Dakota are in the Library of the State Historical Society of North Dakota, at Bismarck. The schedules for Colorado are also available on microfilm.

Information in the records.--The schedules show the same information that the 1880 schedules show except that in a large number of instances the initial letters of the given names of the persons enumerated appear instead of the names.

1890 Schedules (Special Census)

The regular 1890 schedules were destroyed or badly damaged by a fire in Washington on January 10, 1921. Practically all the schedules not then destroyed were destroyed by congressional authorization in 1933. The National Archives, however, has some of the 1890 special census schedules.

The records.--The 1890 special census schedules were created pursuant to section 17 of an act of Congress approved March 1, 1889 (25 Stat. 765), which provided for a census of Union veterans of the Civil War. The extant schedules relate to the States and Territories whose names run alphabetically from Kentucky through Wyoming, but the schedules for Kentucky are incomplete. The schedules are unbound. They are arranged by State or Territory, thereunder by census district, thereunder by county, and thereunder by minor subdivision. These schedules are also available on microfilm.

Information in the records. --Each entry shows the name of a Union veteran of the Civil War (or, if his widow was living, the names of each); the veteran's rank, company, regiment, or vessel; the date of enlistment, date of discharge, and length of service in years, months, and days; the post office address; the nature of the disability if any was incurred; and remarks necessary to complete the statement of the veteran's period of service.

Research aids. --See Evangeline Thurber, "The 1890 Census Records of the Veterans of the Union Army," in National Genealogical Society Quarterly, 34:7-9 (Mar. 1946).

An outline map prepared by the Department of Agriculture shows the name and location of each county in the United States in 1890. The copy in the National Archives is in a binder with other outline maps.

Specialized Information for Each State and Territory

The census years for which schedules are available in the National Archives are given for the States and Territories listed below, often with additional information on these schedules or Federal or State censuses for other years.

Alabama: 1830, 1840, 1850, 1860, 1870, 1880.

The extant part of the Alabama Territorial Census for 1820 is in the State Department of Archives and History, Montgomery. The National Archives Library has a copy as printed in The Alabama Historical Quarterly, volume 6, number 3 (fall, 1944).

Arizona: 1850, 1860, 1864, 1866, 1867, 1869, 1870, 1880.

The schedules for 1850 and 1860 that relate to the present State of Arizona are included among the schedules for New Mexico. The 1864 schedules in the National Archives are in the form of photostats, typed copies, and mimeographed copies of the schedules in the Office of the Secretary of State, Phoenix. The mimeographed copy is an unindexed transcript issued by the Historical Records Survey in 1938. The schedules of 1866, 1867, and 1869 in the National Archives are in the form of photostats and relate only to some counties.

Arkansas: 1830, 1840, 1850, 1860, 1870, 1880.

The 1860 schedules for Little River County are missing.

California: 1850, 1860, 1870, 1880.

The 1850 schedules for Contra Costa, San Francisco, and Santa Clara Counties are missing from the National Archives record set. The Daughters of the American Revolution Library, 1776 D Street, N. W., Washington 6, D. C., has 13 volumes of typed indexed transcripts of the 1852 State census, which were made from the originals in the office of the Secretary of State, Sacramento.

Colorado: 1860, 1870, 1880, 1885.

The 1860 schedules relating to the present State of Colorado are included in the 1860 schedules for Kansas.

Connecticut: 1790, 1800, 1810, 1820, 1830, 1840, 1850, 1860, 1870, 1880.

The 1790 schedules have been printed and indexed in Bureau of the Census, Heads of Families at the First Census of the United States Taken in the year 1790 . . . Connecticut (Washington, 1908).

Dakota: 1860, 1870, 1880. See also North Dakota and South Dakota.

The 1885 schedules prepared by the Territory pursuant to section 22 of an act of Congress approved March 3, 1879 (20 Stat. 480), are in the Library of the State Historical Society of North Dakota, at Bismarck. The schedules are reproduced in Collections of the State Historical Society of North Dakota, 4:338-448 (Fargo, 1913). The names of the persons enumerated are in a general index to the volume.

Delaware: 1800, 1810, 1820, 1830, 1840, 1850, 1860, 1870, 1880.

The missing 1790 census has been reconstructed on the basis of local real estate tax lists and published in Leon de Valinger, Reconstructed 1790 Census of Delaware (Washington, 1954. Genealogical Publications of the National Genealogical Society, vol. 10). Entries for each hundred of each county are arranged alphabetically.

District of Columbia: 1790, 1800, 1820, 1830, 1840, 1850, 1860, 1870, 1880.

Schedules for 1790 that relate to the present District of Columbia are included among the 1790 schedules of Maryland (parts of Montgomery and Prince Georges Counties). Entries for the extant 1800 schedules have been alphabetized and printed in Artemas C. Harmon, "U. S. Census of the District of Columbia in Maryland for the Year 1800," in National Genealogical Society Quarterly, 38:105-110 and 39:16-19, 56-59 (Dec. 1950-June 1951). They cover only the present District of Columbia, which is on the Maryland side of the Potomac River. The 1820, 1830, and 1840 schedules include Alexandria County, the part of the District of Columbia that was retroceded to Virginia.

For the location of the ward boundaries of Washington City and Georgetown for each of the decennial years 1820-70, see Laurence F. Schmeckebier, "Ward Boundaries of Washington and Georgetown," in Records of the Columbia Historical Society, 51-52:66-77, with maps (1955). The National Archives has large-scale copies of these maps.

Florida: 1830, 1840, 1850, 1860, 1870, 1880, 1885.

Georgia: 1820, 1830, 1840, 1850, 1860, 1870, 1880.

Some tax lists for various years for a few of the counties have been published in Georgia, Department of Archives and History, Some Early

Tax Digests of Georgia (Atlanta, 1926). This publication is used as a substitute for schedules missing for the decennial years 1790-1820. The National Archives Library has the publication and the one-volume typed index to it. The Georgia Department of Archives and History, Atlanta, has an enumerator's copy, of which the National Archives has a photostatic copy, of the missing 1800 schedules for Oglethorpe County.

The 1820 schedules for Franklin, Rabun, and Twiggs Counties are not known to be extant.

Idaho: 1870, 1880

Two pages of the 1880 schedules for the Seventh or Lava District of Alturas County were missing from the schedules contemporaneously sent to Washington and were not included on the microfilm made by the Census Bureau. The National Archives, however, has photostats of the originals in the Idaho Historical Society, Boise.

Illinois: 1820, 1830, 1840, 1850, 1860, 1870, 1880.

Part of the 1810 schedules, apparently for Randolph County alone, are in the Illinois State Library, Springfield. These schedules together with 1818 schedules for Illinois Territory were transcribed and published in Collections of the Illinois State Historical Library, vol. 24 (1935). The 1820 State schedules, which differ slightly from the 1820 Federal schedules, have been published in Collections of the Illinois State Historical Library, vol. 26 (1934). These publications are in the National Archives Library.

The Illinois State Library, Springfield, has a master card index which includes the names on most of the schedules for 1830 and 1840 and some of the schedules for 1850.

The 1850 schedules for Edgar County show the county of birth of each person enumerated. See articles by O. Kenneth Baker in National Genealogical Society Quarterly, 36:73-76 (Sept. 1948), 38:1-5 (Mar. 1950), and 38:41-46 (June 1950).

For information about State censuses for the years 1835, 1845, 1855, and 1865, see the appendix to Library of Congress, Census Library Project, State Censuses, p. 67-68 (Washington, 1948).

Indiana: 1820, 1830, 1840, 1850, 1860, 1870, 1880.

The Genealogical Division, Indiana State Library, Indianapolis, has indexes to the 1820 and 1830 Indiana schedules. Printed transcripts of the 1830 schedules for Marion County appear in Indiana Historical Society Publications, 4: 339-371 (1908).

Iowa: 1840, 1850, 1860, 1870, 1880.

For information about Territorial and State censuses, 1838-1925, see Library of Congress, Census Library Project, State Censuses, p. 68-69 (Washington, 1948).

Kansas: 1860, 1870, 1880.

For information about Territorial and State Censuses, 1855-1915, see

Library of Congress, Census Library Project, State Censuses, p. 69 (Washington, 1948).

Kentucky: 1810, 1820, 1830, 1840, 1850, 1860, 1870, 1880, 1890 special census.

Schedules for 1790 and 1800 have been reconstructed on the basis of local tax returns. Entries have been alphabetized and printed in two separate volumes as follows: Charles Brunk Heinemann and Gaius Marcus Brumbaugh, "First Census" of Kentucky, 1790 (Washington, 1940); and Garrett Glenn Clift, comp., "Second Census" of Kentucky, 1800 (Frankfort, 1954).

The Filson Club, 118 West Breckinridge Street, Louisville, Ky., reports that it has an index to the 1810 schedules for Kentucky.

The National Archives Library has indexed transcripts of the 1830 schedules for Daviess County.

The 1890 special census is missing for some counties.

Louisiana: 1810, 1820, 1830, 1840, 1850, 1860, 1870, 1880, 1890 special census.

The major subdivisions within the State are known as parishes instead of counties. The National Archives Library has an indexed transcript of the 1850 schedules for Washington Parish.

Maine: 1790, 1800, 1810, 1820, 1830, 1840, 1850, 1860, 1870, 1880, 1890 special census.

The 1790 schedules have been printed and indexed in Bureau of the Census, Heads of Families at the First Census of the United States Taken in the Year 1790 . . . Maine (Washington, 1908).

Part of the 1800 schedules for York County are missing.

Maryland: 1790, 1800, 1810, 1820, 1830, 1840, 1850, 1860, 1870, 1880, 1890 special census.

The 1790 schedules have been printed and indexed in Bureau of the Census, Heads of Families at the First Census of the United States Taken in the Year 1790 . . . Maryland (Washington, 1907).

The Library of the National Society of the Daughters of the American Revolution, 1776 D Street, N. W., Washington 6, D. C., has unindexed typed transcripts of the 1800 schedules in 19 volumes, one for each county.

The 1830 schedules for Montgomery, Prince Georges, Saint Marys, Queen Annes, and Somerset Counties are missing.

Massachusetts: 1790, 1800, 1810, 1820, 1830, 1840, 1850, 1860, 1870, 1880, 1890 special census.

The 1790 schedules have been printed and indexed in Bureau of the Census, Heads of Families at the First Census of the United States Taken in the Year 1790 . . . Massachusetts (Washington, 1908).

Michigan: 1820, 1830, 1840, 1850, 1860, 1870, 1880, 1890 special census.

Minnesota: 1850, 1857, 1860, 1870, 1880, 1890 special census.

A large part of the 1870 schedules formerly in the possession of the Bureau of the Census were destroyed by fire on January 10, 1921; others that were damaged were destroyed by authorization of Congress in 1933. The destroyed schedules concern the counties with names running alphabetically from Aitkin to Sibley. The National Archives has a microfilm copy of the duplicate set of the 1870 schedules in the custody of the Minnesota Historical Society, St. Paul. The society has State schedules for the years 1865, 1875, 1885, 1895, and 1905.

Mississippi: 1820, 1830, 1840, 1850, 1860, 1870, 1880, 1890 special census.

The Mississippi Department of Archives and History, Jackson, has the Territorial schedules for 1816 and some other years. Part of the 1816 schedules have been published in the December 1945 (33:104) and later issues of the National Genealogical Society Quarterly.

The 1830 schedules for Pike County, the 1860 schedules for free and slave inhabitants for Hancock and Washington Counties, and the 1860 schedules for free inhabitants for Tallahatchie County are missing.

Missouri: 1830, 1840, 1850, 1860, 1870, 1880, 1890 special census.

The National Archives Library has alphabetized transcripts of the schedules of Jackson County for 1830 and 1840.

Montana: 1860, 1870, 1880, 1890 special census.

The 1860 schedules that relate to the present State of Montana are included in the volume for the unorganized part of Nebraska Territory.

Nebraska: 1860, 1870, 1880, 1885, 1890 special census.

Nevada: 1860, 1870, 1880, 1890 special census.

The 1860 schedules that relate to the present State of Nevada are included in the volume for Utah.

New Hampshire: 1790, 1800, 1810, 1820, 1830, 1840, 1850, 1860, 1870, 1880, 1890 special census.

The 1790 schedules have been printed and indexed in Bureau of the Census, Heads of Families at the First Census of the United States Taken in the Year 1790 . . . New Hampshire (Washington, 1907).

Part of the 1800 schedules for Rockingham and Strafford Counties and the 1820 schedules for Grafton County are missing.

New Jersey: 1830, 1840, 1850, 1860, 1870, 1880, 1890 special census.

The Library of the National Society of the Daughters of the American Revolution, 1776 D Street, N. W., Washington 6, D. C., has 24 rolls of microfilm containing county tax lists for 1783. The microfilm, which was supplied by the New Jersey State Chairman of Genealogical Records, serves as a partial substitute for the missing 1790 schedules.

The New Jersey State Library, Trenton, has bound volumes of State censuses for the decennial years 1855-1915.

New Mexico: 1850, 1860, 1870, 1880, 1885, 1890 special census.

New York: 1790, 1800, 1810, 1820, 1830, 1840, 1850, 1860, 1870, 1880, 1890 special census.

The 1790 schedules have been printed and indexed in Bureau of the Census, Heads of Families at the First Census of the United States Taken in the Year 1790 . . . New York (Washington, 1908).

Two separate enumerations were taken for New York City in 1870.

Information about State schedules, 1825-1925, for New York was printed in a leaflet prepared in 1942 by the New York State Library and entitled An Inventory of New York State and Federal Census Records. The National Archives Library has an annotated copy.

North Carolina: 1790, 1800, 1810, 1820, 1830, 1840, 1850, 1860, 1870, 1880, 1890 special census.

The 1790 schedules have been printed and indexed in Bureau of the Census, Heads of Families at the First Census of the United States Taken in the Year 1790 . . . North Carolina (Washington, 1908), and in North Carolina, Census (of North Carolina) 1790 Names of Heads of Families (Goldsboro, 1905. The State Records of North Carolina, vol. 26). The 1790 schedules for Caswell, Granville, and Orange counties are not extant. In their places in the above volumes are transcripts of local tax lists.

The 1810 schedules for Craven, Greene, New Hanover, and Wake Counties and the 1820 schedules for Currituck, Franklin, Martin, Montgomery, Randolph, and Wake Counties are missing.

North Dakota: 1890 special census. See also Dakota.

The Library of the State Historical Society of North Dakota, at Bismarck, has State census schedules for 1915 and 1925.

Ohio: 1820, 1830, 1840, 1850, 1860, 1870, 1880, 1890 special census.

The National Archives Library has an indexed transcript of the 1820 schedules for Trumbull County and an index to the 1820 schedules for Clermont and Wayne Counties.

Oklahoma or Indian Territory: 1860, 1890 special census.

The 1860 schedules that relate to the present State of Oklahoma are bound under Arkansas, volume 8. The persons enumerated were dwelling on Indian lands.

The 1890 Territorial census schedules, with a card index, are in the Oklahoma Historical Society, Oklahoma City.

Oregon: 1850, 1860, 1870, 1880, 1890 special census.

The index in Oregon State Library, State Archives Division, Pioneer Families of the Oregon Territory (1951), includes an index to the 1850 schedules. The Territorial schedules for 1845 and 1849 are in the custody of the Oregon Historical Society, Portland.

Pennsylvania: 1790, 1800, 1810, 1820, 1830, 1840, 1850, 1860, 1870, 1880, 1890 special census.

The 1790 schedules have been printed and indexed in Bureau of the Census, Heads of Families at the First Census of the United States Taken in the Year 1790 . . . Pennsylvania (Washington, 1908).

Rhode Island: 1790, 1800, 1810, 1820, 1830, 1840, 1850, 1860, 1870, 1880, 1890 special census.

The 1790 schedules have been printed and indexed in Bureau of the Census, Heads of Families at the First Census of the United States Taken in the Year 1790 . . . Rhode Island (Washington, 1908).

For information about decennial State schedules, 1865-1925, see the appendix to Library of Congress, Census Library Project, State Censuses (Washington, 1948).

South Carolina: 1790, 1800, 1820, 1830, 1840, 1850, 1860, 1870, 1880, 1890 special census.

The 1790 schedules for South Carolina have been printed and indexed in Bureau of the Census, Heads of Families at the First Census of the United States Taken in the Year 1790 . . . South Carolina (Washington, 1908).

The schedules of Clarendon County for the decennial years 1820-50 are missing.

The National Archives Library has an indexed transcript of the 1800 schedules for Laurens County.

For information about counties and districts in South Carolina and their boundaries see Roberta Wakefield, "Evolution of South Carolina Counties," in National Genealogical Society Quarterly, 32:51-52 (June 1944).

South Dakota: See Dakota.

The South Dakota Historical Society, Pierre, has State census schedules for 1905, 1915, 1925, and 1935.

Tennessee: 1810 (Grainger and Rutherford Counties), 1820, 1830, 1840 1850, 1860, 1870, 1880, 1890 special census.

Some of the 1800 schedules have been reconstructed from local tax records. See the series, "Early East Tennessee Tax Payers," by Pollyanna Creekmore in The East Tennessee Historical Society's Publications: Anderson County, No. 23 (1951); Blount County, No. 24 (1952); Knox County, No. 26 (1954); Grainger County, No. 27 (1955); Jefferson County, No. 28 (1956); Carter County, No. 30 (1958); and Sullivan County, No. 31 (1959).

The National Archives has the 1810 schedules for Rutherford County and the 1820 schedules for 26 of the 48 counties; namely, Bedford, Davidson, Dickson, Franklin, Giles, Hardin, Hawkins, Humphreys, Jackson, Lawrence, Lincoln, Maury, Montgomery, Overton, Perry, Robertson, Rutherford, Shelby, Smith, Stewart, Sumner, Warren, Wayne, White, Williamson, and Wilson. The McClung Historical Collection, Lawson McGhee Library, Knoxville, includes the enumerator's copy for part of the 1810 schedules for Grainger County. No other Tennessee schedules for these census years are known. The extant 1810 and 1820 schedules in the National Archives have been transcribed and indexed by the Tennessee State Library and Archives and published in a 27-volume series, Tennessee Census Reports (Washington, 1933-36). The 1810 schedules for Grainger County have been transcribed and published in Pollyanna Creekmore, Grainger County, Tennessee Federal Census of 1810, Population Schedule (Third Census) and County Tax Lists for 1810 (Knoxville, 1956. McClung Historical Collection Special Studies No. 1). The National Archives Library has these publications for Rutherford and Grainger Counties, 1810, and for Davidson and Dickson Counties, 1820.

The National Archives Library has indexed transcripts of the 1830 schedules for Giles and Sevier Counties; the 1850 schedules for Bedford, Sevier, and Smith Counties; and the 1870 schedules for Smith County.

Texas: 1850, 1860, 1870, 1880, 1890 special census.

The Texas State Archives, Austin, has the extant Texas census schedules for 1829-36. They are being reprinted in a series by Marion Day Mullins, "The First Census of Texas, 1829-1836," in the June 1952 (40:49) and later issues of National Genealogical Society Quarterly.

Utah: 1850, 1860, 1870, 1880, 1890 special census.

Vermont: 1790, 1800, 1810, 1820, 1830, 1840, 1850, 1860, 1870, 1880, 1890 special census.

The 1790 schedules have been printed and indexed in Bureau of the Census, Heads of Families at the First Census of the United States Taken in the Year 1790 . . . Vermont (Washington, 1907).

The 1800 schedules have been printed and indexed in Census Office, 2d Census, 1800, Heads of Families at the Second Census of the United States Taken in the Year 1800: Vermont (Montpelier, 1938).

Virginia: 1800 (Accomac County), 1810, 1820, 1830, 1840, 1850, 1860, 1870, 1880, 1890 special census.

The 1790 schedules have been reconstructed and published in two volumes that supplement each other: Bureau of the Census, Heads of Families at the First Census of the United States Taken in the Year 1790 [based on] Records of the State Enumerations: 1782 to 1785 Virginia (Washington, 1908), and Augusta B. Fothergill and John Mark Naugle, Virginia Tax Papers, 1782-87, Other Than Those Published by the United States Census Bureau (Richmond, 1940).

The National Archives Library has a photostat copy of the 1800 enumerator's returns for Accomac County. The originals are in the Virginia State Library, Richmond.

The 1810 schedules for the following counties are missing: Grayson, Greenbrier, Halifax, Hardy, Henry, James City, King William, Louisa, Mecklenburg, Nansemond, Northampton, Orange, Patrick, Pittsylvania, Russell, and Tazewell.

The National Archives Library has indexed transcripts of the 1810 schedules for Randolph County and alphabetized transcripts of the 1810 schedules for Brooke County.

Washington: 1860, 1870, 1880, 1890 special census.

The 1860 schedules for Benton, Columbia, San Juan, and Snokomish Counties and the 1870 schedules for Benton and Columbia Counties are missing.

West Virginia: 1870, 1880, 1890 special census. For earlier censuses, see Virginia.

Wisconsin: 1820, 1830, 1840, 1850, 1860, 1870, 1880, 1890 special census.

The schedules for 1820 and 1830 are included under Michigan.

The State Historical Society of Wisconsin, Madison, has indexes to the Wisconsin schedules for the decennial years 1820-70. It also has Territorial or State schedules for 1836, 1838, 1842, 1846, 1847, 1855, 1865, 1875, 1885, 1895, and 1905. The 1905 schedules, which are on microfilm, are the only State schedules to show the names of all members of each family.

Wyoming: 1860, 1870, 1880, 1890 special census.

The 1860 schedules that relate to the present State of Wyoming are included in the schedules for Nebraska.

The Library of Congress has typed, indexed transcripts of the 1870 and 1880 schedules under the titles U. S. Census Office, 9th Census, 1870 [Census of Wyoming, 1870] (1925); and U. S. Census Office, 10th Census, 1880 [1880 Census, Wyoming Territory] (Cheyenne, 1927).

Suggestions and General Information for Research in Population Census Schedules

Searches for Place of Residence

The indexed 1790 schedules are of the greatest use genealogically because they show where persons of each surname were residing. If over 100 persons of any surname are listed in 1790, information about their geographical distribution by name of State appears in Bureau of the Census, A Century of Population Growth, 1790-1900 (Washington, 1909).

If a searcher knows only the name of the State in which a person was living after 1790, the search in many instances is apt to be so time consuming as to be prohibitive. It is usually necessary to know the name of the city or county of residence before a search can be confined within reasonable limits.

Schedules for counties. --In tracing a family name through the census schedules, a searcher often finds that the name of a county in one set of schedules is lacking in the next. This situation results from the fact that as population increased, the older counties were broken up and new counties were formed from them. F. Douglas Halverson has prepared a useful though not completely accurate checklist showing by State or Territory the name of each county, the date of its formation, the name of the parent county, and the name of the county seat. This checklist is reprinted in E. Kay Kirkham, Research in American Genealogy, p. 114-203 (Salt Lake City, 1956), a copy of which is in the National Archives Library. The National Archives also has various maps and atlases that will assist the searcher in determining the geographical extent of a county over varying periods of time.

In the North the inhabitants of the individual counties are so numerous that it is often advisable to ascertain the name of the township, town, or other subdivision before a search is begun. Such information can often be gleaned from local records.

Schedules for cities.--The schedules for a city are so numerous that a searcher will usually find it advisable to ascertain the number of the ward in which a person lived before beginning a search. This can be done by the combined use of a contemporary city directory and a contemporary map. It is important to use such tools that were made within a year or two of the census year, because ward numbers and boundaries frequently changed and persons often moved. As the schedules before 1880 do not normally show street numbers, the searches are often difficult.

The first step in a search is to locate a contemporary city directory from which to ascertain the name of the street on which a person lived. If the appropriate city directory cannot be located in the National Archives, research can be made in the large collection of city directories in the Library of Congress. A checklist of these directories in the Library of Congress prepared by Philip M. Smith was published in the July 1936 issue of American Genealogist (13:46-53) and was corrected in the July 1951 issue (27:142). A corrected photostat copy of the July 1936 issue is in the National Archives Library.

The second step is to locate a contemporary map showing ward boundaries and street names so as to identify the number of the ward or the numbers of the wards in which the street was located. The National Archives has many city maps. It also has a copy of E. Kay Kirkham, Research in American Genealogy (Salt Lake City, 1956), which includes "A Select Bibliography of Available Maps and City Directories of Some of the Larger Cities of the United States" (p. 96-107). The maps in this bibliography have been microfilmed on a roll that is in the National Archives. If an adequate map is not available in the National Archives, the searcher should consult the Map Division, Library of Congress Annex, Washington, D. C.

Checklists for Finding the Volume Needed

For the volume number of the extant schedules relating to each county, 1800-70, see National Archives, Population Schedules, 1800-1870; Volume Index to Counties and Major Cities (Washington, 1951). For the microfilm roll number of the 1840-80 schedules relating to each county (the 1880 ones are available only on microfilm), see National Archives, Federal Population Censuses, 1840-80; a Price List of Microfilm Copies of the Original Schedules (Washington, 1955). For the extant 1890 special schedules relating to each county, see the typed "Preliminary Checklist of Schedules of the 1890 Census Enumerating Union Veterans and Widows of Union Veterans of the Civil War," prepared in May 1945 by the National Archives.

Pagination of the Volumes of the Schedules for the Decennial Years 1800-70

Many of the schedules contain two or more series of page numbers. The series cited by the National Archives is the series that runs consecutively throughout each volume used in the Central Research Room, whether photostat or original.

In some volumes a hand stamp was used for numbering and only alternate pages are numbered. In such instances the National Archives refers to the right-hand page as the "face" and the back of the page as the "reverse."

As microfilm or other copies of the schedules do not necessarily have the same pagination, it is wise, in citing a reference, to give not only the volume number, page number, and name of the State, but also the name of the county and the minor subdivision.

Copies of Census Schedules Outside the National Archives

The preparation of two sets of the population census schedules for the decennial years 1830-80 was required by law. The duplicate sets for 1830 and 1840 were filed with the Federal district or superior courts. The duplicate sets for 1850, 1860, 1870, and 1880 were filed with the county courts. Many schedules filed with the county courts have been deposited in State libraries or State archives.

The Federal set of the 1880 schedules, which were in very fragile condition, were transferred to various non-Federal depositories in 1956.

Many libraries having genealogical collections have sets of the published 1790 schedules and microfilm copies of some of the 19th-century schedules. The National Archives has a file of filled-out questionnaires identifying the census holdings in 1957 of a number of the larger libraries, archives, and historical societies.

MORTALITY CENSUS SCHEDULES

The mortality schedules for 1850, 1860, 1870, 1880, and 1885 were based on schedule 6 as outlined in an act of Congress approved May 23, 1850 (9 Stat. 436). The schedules relate to persons dying in the United States during the 12 months preceding the taking of the census. The mortality schedules for 1885 only are in the National Archives.

1850-80 Schedules

Information for the mortality schedules for the decennial years 1850, 1860, 1870, and 1880 was taken as of June 1 of each decennial year. The schedules were distributed by the Bureau of the Census to non-Federal depositories in 1918 and 1919. Information as to the distribution of the schedules for each State or Territory appears in an article entitled "The 'Mortality Schedules,'" in National Genealogical Society Quarterly,

31:45-49 (June 1943). Following is a list showing the schedules that were given to the Library of the Daughters of the American Revolution, 1776 D Street N. W., Washington 25, D. C., with notations showing which have been indexed, or transcribed and indexed:

Arizona: 1870; 1880
Colorado: 1870; 1880
District of Columbia: 1850; 1860; 1870; 1880
Georgia: 1850, indexed; 1860, indexed; 1870, indexed; 1880
Kentucky: 1850; 1860, indexed; 1870, indexed; 1880, transcribed and indexed
Louisiana: 1850, indexed; 1860, indexed; 1870, indexed; 1880, transcribed and indexed
Tennessee: 1850, indexed; 1860, indexed; 1880

1885 Schedules

The records.--The mortality schedules for 1885 were created under terms of section 22 of an act of Congress approved March 3, 1879 (20 Stat. 480). This section provided that the Federal Government would pay the States or Territories approximately one-half the cost of taking a semi-decennial census in 1885. The States or Territories of Colorado, Dakota, Florida, Nebraska, and New Mexico took advantage of this offer; the mortality schedules for all but Dakota are in the National Archives. The schedules for Colorado are also available on microfilm.

Information in the records.--For each person who died during the 12 months preceding June 1, 1885, an entry shows the name, age, sex, and color; marital status; the State, Territory, or country of birth; the month of death; occupation; and the cause of death.

GENERAL OBSERVATIONS

History of Federal Census

Detailed information about each population, mortality, and other census, 1790-1890, appears in Carroll D. Wright, The History and Growth of the United States Census, 1790-1890 (Washington, 1900), 56th Cong., 1st sess., S. Doc. 194, Serial 3,856.

Purchase of Microfilm

For information about the purchase of microfilm copies of the 1830 population schedules, the 1890 special schedules, the 1885 population and mortality schedules for Colorado, and some other population schedules, 1800-20, see National Archives, List of National Archives Microfilm Publications, p. 143-153, 154-159 (Washington, 1961). For information about the purchase of copies of the population schedules for the decennial years 1840-80, see National Archives, Federal Population Censuses, 1840-80; a Price List of Microfilm Copies of the Original Schedules (Washington, 1955). The National Archives, Washington 25, D.C., sells microfilm copies of the 1790 schedules as printed by the Government Printing Office.

Record Groups

The records are in Record Group 29, Records of the Bureau of the Census, except for the schedules for the special census for 1890, which are in Record Group 15, Records of the Veterans Administration.

II. PASSENGER ARRIVAL LISTS

The passenger arrival lists in the National Archives record names of passengers arriving from abroad at ports on the Atlantic Ocean or the Gulf of Mexico and a few inland ports. Although there are lists for as early as 1798, most of them are for the years 1820-1945, and for those years there are many gaps. The San Francisco passenger lists were destroyed by fires in 1851 and 1940, and lists for other Pacific coast ports, if they exist, have not been transferred to the National Archives. During the 19th century the law did not require passenger arrival records as such to be kept for persons entering the United States by land from Canada and Mexico.

The lists consist of customs passenger lists, customs lists of aliens, and immigration passenger lists. The National Archives has customs lists of aliens for only the ports of Salem and Beverly, Mass. The following table shows the ports for which there are customs and immigration passenger lists, the kinds of lists for each port, and their dates. In general, gaps of more than a year are shown in the dates given, but the lists are not necessarily complete for the year or years shown. The kinds of lists are described below.

PORTS OR CUSTOMS DISTRICTS FOR WHICH THE NATIONAL ARCHIVES HAS PASSENGER LISTS, SHOWING DATES FOR EACH TYPE OF LIST

Name of port or district	Customs passenger lists			Immigration passenger lists
	Originals	Copies and abstracts	State Department transcripts	
Alexandria, Va.[1]	----------	1820-52	1820-31	------------------------
Annapolis, Md.	----------	1849	----------------	------------------------
Apalachicola, Fla.	----------	--------------	----------------	Sept. 4, 1918
Baltimore, Md.	1820-91	1820-69	1820, 1822-27, 1829	Dec. 12, 1891-Nov. 30,1909
Bangor, Maine	----------	1848	----------------	------------------------
Barnstable, Mass.	----------	1820-26	1820-26	------------------------
Bath, Maine	----------	1825-32, 1867	----------------	------------------------
Beaufort, N. C.	----------	1865	----------------	------------------------
Belfast, Maine	----------	1820-31, 1851	1820, 1822-24; 1827, 1829, 1831	------------------------
Boca Grande, Fla.	----------	--------------	----------------	Oct. 28, 1912-Aug. 16, 1935
Boston and Charlestown, Mass.	1883-99	1820-74	1820-27	Aug. 1, 1891-Dec. 1943

[1] There are also cargo manifests for Alexandria, 1798-1819, that contain names of some passengers.

747-596 O - 64 - 3

PORTS OR CUSTOMS DISTRICTS FOR WHICH THE NATIONAL ARCHIVES HAS PASSENGER LISTS, SHOWING DATES FOR EACH TYPE OF LIST--Continued

Name of port or district	Customs passenger lists			Immigration passenger lists
	Originals	Copies and abstracts	State Department transcripts	
Bridgeport, Conn.	----------	1870	----------------	------------------------
Bridgetown, N. J.	----------	1828	1828	------------------------
Bristol and Warren, R. I.	----------	1820-24, 1828, 1843-71	1820-28	------------------------
Brunswick, Ga.	----------	-------------	----------------	Nov. 22, 1901 - Nov. 27, 1939
Cape May, N. J.	----------	1828	----------------	------------------------
Carabelle, Fla.	----------	-------------	----------------	Nov. 7. 1915
Charleston, S. C. [2]	----------	1820-29	1820-29	Apr. 9, 1906-Dec. 3, 1945
Darien, Ga.	----------	1823, 1825	----------------	------------------------
Dighton, Mass.	----------	1820-36	1819, 1823, 1826, 1828	------------------------
East River, Va.	----------	1830	1830	------------------------
Edenton, N. C.	----------	1820	1820	------------------------

[2]Sometimes shown in the customs records as the District of South Carolina.

Edgartown, Mass.	----------	1820-70	1820-28, 1831-32	------------------------
Fairfield, Conn.	----------	1820-21	1820	------------------------
Fall River, Mass.	----------	1837-65	----------------	------------------------
Fernandina, Fla.	----------	--------------	----------------	Aug. 29, 1904-Oct. 7, 1932
Frenchman's Bay, Maine	----------	1821, 1826, 1827	1822, 1825-27	------------------------
Galveston, Tex.	----------	1846-71	----------------	------------------------
Georgetown, D. C.	----------	1820-21	1820	------------------------
Georgetown, S. C.	----------	--------------	----------------	June 17, 1923-Oct. 24, 1939
Gloucester, Mass.	----------	1820, 1832-39, 1867-70	----------------	Oct. 1906-June 1923, Feb. 1, 1930-Dec. 1943
Gulfport, Miss.	----------	--------------	----------------	Aug. 1904-Sept. 1944
Hampton, Va.	----------	1821	----------------	------------------------
Hartford, Conn.	----------	1832	----------------	Feb. 1929-Dec. 1943
Havre de Grace, Md.	----------	1820	----------------	------------------------
Hingham, Mass.	----------	1852	----------------	------------------------
Jacksonville, Fla.[3]	----------	--------------	----------------	Jan. 18, 1904-Dec. 17, 1945

[3] At least one passenger list for Jacksonville, that of Feb. 24, 1916, is filed with those for Mayport.

PORTS OR CUSTOMS DISTRICTS FOR WHICH THE NATIONAL ARCHIVES HAS PASSENGER LISTS, SHOWING DATES FOR EACH TYPE OF LIST--Continued

Name of port or district	Customs passenger lists			Immigration passenger lists
	Originals	Copies and abstracts	State Department transcripts	
Kennebunk, Maine	----------	1820-27, 1842	1820, 1822-25, 1827	----------
Key West, Fla.	----------	1837-68	----------	Nov. 1898-Dec. 1945
Knights Key, Fla.	----------	----------	----------	Feb. 7, 1908-Jan. 20, 1912
Little Egg Harbor (port of Tuckerton), N. J.	----------	1831	----------	----------
Marblehead, Mass.	----------	1820-52	1821-23, 1825-27	----------
Mayport, Fla.	----------	----------	----------	Nov. 16, 1907-Apr. 13, 1916
Miami, Fla.	----------	----------	----------	Oct. 1899-Dec. 1945
Millville, Fla.	----------	----------	----------	July 4, 1916
Mobile, Ala.	1820-62	1832, 1849-52	----------	Apr. 3, 1904-Dec. 24, 1945
Nantucket, Mass.	----------	1820-62	1820, 1822-25, 1829, 1831	----------
New Bedford, Mass.	1823-99	1826-52	1822, 1825-27, 1830-31	July 1, 1902-July 1942

New Bern, N. C.	----------	1820-45, 1865	1820-30	------------------------
New Haven, Conn.	----------	1820-73	1822-31	------------------------
New London, Conn.	----------	1820-47	1820, 1823-27, 1829, 1831	------------------------
New Orleans, La.	1820-1902	1820-75	1820-27	Jan. 1903-Dec. 1945
New York, N. Y.	1820-97	1820-74	1820-27	June 16, 1897-1942
Newark, N. J.	----------	1836	----------------	------------------------
Newburyport, Mass.	----------	1821-39	1821-31	------------------------
Newport, R. I.	1820-75	1820-57	1820-28, 1830-31	------------------------
Norfolk and Portsmouth, Va.	----------	1820-57	1820-32	------------------------
Oswegatchie, N. Y.	----------	1821-23	1821-23	------------------------
Panama City, Fla.	----------	--------------	----------------	Nov. 10, 1927-Dec. 12,1939
Pascagoula, Miss.	----------	--------------	----------------	July 15, 1903-May 21, 1935
Passamaquoddy, Maine	----------	1820-59	1822-26, 1831	------------------------
Penobscot, Maine	----------	1851	----------------	------------------------
Pensacola, Fla.	----------	--------------	----------------	May 12, 1900-July 16, 1945
Perth Amboy, N. J.	----------	1820, 1829-32	1829	------------------------

PORTS OR CUSTOMS DISTRICTS FOR WHICH THE NATIONAL ARCHIVES HAS PASSENGER LISTS, SHOWING DATES FOR EACH TYPE OF LIST--Continued

Name of port or district	Customs passenger lists			Immigration passenger lists
	Originals	Copies and abstracts	State Department transcripts	
Petersburg, Va.	----------	1820-21	1819-20, 1822	------------------------
Philadelphia, Pa.[4]	1820-99	1820-54	1820-22, 1824-27, 1829	Jan. 1883-Dec. 31, 1945
Plymouth, Mass.	----------	1821-43	1822, 1824, 1826-27, 1829-30	------------------------
Plymouth, N. C.	----------	1820, 1825, 1840	1820, 1823	------------------------
Port Everglades, Fla.	----------	--------------	----------------	Feb. 15, 1932-Dec. 10, 1945
Port Inglis, Fla.	----------	--------------	----------------	Mar. 29, 1912, Jan. 2, 1913
Port Royal, S. C.	----------	1865	----------------	------------------------
Port St. Joe, Fla.	----------	--------------	----------------	Jan. 12, 1923-Oct. 13, 1939
Portland and Falmouth, Maine	----------	1820-68, 1873	1820-32	Nov. 1893-Mar. 1943
Portsmouth, N. H.	----------	1820-61	1820, 1822, 1824-31	------------------------
Providence, R. I.	----------	1820-67	1820, 1822-31	June 1911-June 1943

[4] There are also cargo manifests for Philadelphia, 1800-19, that contain names of passengers.

Richmond, Va.	----------	1820-44	1820-24, 1828, 1830	------------------------
Rochester, N. Y.	----------	1866	----------------	------------------------
Sag Harbor, N. Y.	----------	1829-34	1829	------------------------
St. Andrews, Fla.	----------	--------------	----------------	Jan. 2, 1916-May 13, 1926
St. Augustine, Fla.	----------	1821-27, 1870	1822-24, 1827	------------------------
St. Johns, Fla.	----------	1865	----------------	------------------------
St. Petersburg, Fla.	----------	--------------	----------------	Dec. 15, 1926-March 1, 1941
Salem and Beverly, Mass.[5]	----------	1865-66	1823	------------------------
Sandusky, Ohio	----------	1820	1820	------------------------
Savannah, Ga.	----------	1820-68	1820-23, 1825-26, 1831	June 5, 1906-Dec. 6, 1945
Saybrook, Conn.	----------	1820	----------------	------------------------
Tampa, Fla.	----------	--------------	----------------	Nov. 1898-Dec. 1945
Waldoboro, Maine	----------	1820-33	1820-21	------------------------
Washington, N. C.	----------	1820-48	1828-29, 1831	------------------------
West Palm Beach, Fla.	----------	--------------	----------------	Sept. 8, 1920-Nov. 21, 1945

[5]There are also customs lists of aliens arriving at these ports, 1798-1800.

PORTS OR CUSTOMS DISTRICTS FOR WHICH THE NATIONAL ARCHIVES HAS PASSENGER LISTS, SHOWING DATES FOR EACH TYPE OF LIST--Continued

Name of port or district	Customs passenger lists			Immigration passenger lists
	Originals	Copies and abstracts	State Department transcripts	
Wilmington, Del.[6]	----------	1820-48	1820	------------------------
Wiscasset, Maine	----------	--------------	1819, 1829	------------------------
Yarmouth, Maine	----------	1820	----------------	------------------------

[6] The State Department transcripts are entered under the District of Delaware.

CUSTOMS PASSENGER LISTS

The records known as customs passenger lists were filed by the masters of ships with collectors of customs in compliance with an act of Congress approved March 2, 1819 (3 Stat. 489), and later acts. The National Archives has customs passenger lists for the period 1819-1902. Besides the original lists, which are dated 1820-1902, there are copies and abstracts, 1820-75, and transcripts, 1819-32. Each of these forms of the lists is described below.

If the original lists are available either on paper or as microfilm copies, their use is to be preferred over that of handwritten copies, abstracts, and transcripts because of the possibility of error in transcribing. Although the indexes may contain the desired information about the arrival of a passenger, because of the possibility of error the information should be verified on the original list if possible.

Microfilm Copies

As time and resources permit, the National Archives is microfilming the customs passenger lists. The goal is to give as complete coverage as possible for a port up to the beginning date of the microfilm copies of immigration passenger lists for that port. The following projects except Philadelphia have been completed.

Baltimore. --Passenger lists for Baltimore, 1820-91, have been microfilmed. Original lists for that port created in compliance with Maryland law, 1833-66, were borrowed from the city of Baltimore and microfilmed to fill gaps in the Federal passenger lists. An index to the Federal passenger lists for Baltimore, 1820-97, and an index to the city passenger lists, 1833-66, have also been microfilmed.

Boston. --Original passenger lists for Boston, 1883-91, and copies of lists for Boston, 1820-74, have been microfilmed. An index to the passenger lists that were made in compliance with Massachusetts law, 1848-91, has also been microfilmed.

New Orleans. --The original passenger lists for New Orleans, 1820-1902, have been microfilmed, and a separate microcopy has been made of the abstracts of the lists for that port, 1820-75.

New York. --The customs passenger lists for New York have been microfilmed for the period 1820 to June 17, 1897. When the original lists were prepared for microfilming, copies of them, if available, were substituted for originals that were missing or were in poor physical condition. An index to copies of the New York lists, 1820-46, has also been microfilmed.

Philadelphia. --Cargo manifests for 1800-19 and a few of later date containing names of passengers that do not appear on the customs passenger lists are being filmed with the passenger lists to make the coverage as complete as possible for the years 1800-82. Filming of the index to the lists and manifests, 1800-1906, has been completed.

Original Lists

The records. --There are original lists for only a few ports: Baltimore, Boston, New Bedford, New Orleans, New York, and Philadelphia, with a few for Mobile. The lists for most of these ports do not cover the entire period 1820-1902.

Information in the records.--The original lists were prepared on board ship, sworn to by the master of the ship, and filed with the collector of customs when the ship arrived at the port. They usually contain the following information: name of vessel, name of master, name of the port of embarkation, date of arrival, and name of the port of arrival; and for each passenger, his name, age, sex, and occupation, name of the country to which he belonged, name of the country that he intended to inhabit, and, if he died en route, the date or circumstances of his death.

Baltimore Lists

The records.--The Baltimore lists are dated 1820-91.

Indexes.--There are three separate indexes in the National Archives to the names on the lists of passengers arriving at the port of Baltimore. One is an index to the names on the lists made in compliance with Federal law, which covers the period 1832-97, with a few entries for arrivals as early as 1820. Another is an index to the names on the lists made in compliance with Maryland law and on deposit in the City Hall in Baltimore. This index, better known as the "City Index," covers the period 1833-66. Both indexes were transferred to the National Archives from the Baltimore District Office of the Immigration and Naturalization Service. They are both arranged according to the Soundex filing system; that is, alphabetically by the first letter of the surname of the passenger, thereunder by the sound of the surname, and thereunder alphabetically by given name. Entries are located through the use of a code. The third index is the index to the copies of lists for Atlantic and gulf coast ports exclusive of New York, described below.

Boston Lists

The records.--The Boston lists are dated 1883-99. Earlier original lists were reportedly destroyed in a fire in 1894.

Index.--The National Archives has an alphabetical index to names on passenger lists filed at Boston in compliance with Massachusetts law, 1848-91, and now in the Archives Division, Office of the Secretary of the Commonwealth, Boston. The index was prepared by the Work Projects Administration for the Immigration and Naturalization Service. It serves as a partial index to the names on the customs passenger lists for Boston in the National Archives.

Mobile Lists

The records.--The Mobile lists are dated 1820-62, with a few as late as 1884. There are very few lists for some years and none for others.

Index.--The index to the copies of lists for Atlantic and gulf coast ports exclusive of New York, described below, serves as an index to the original lists for Mobile.

New Bedford Lists

The records.--The New Bedford lists are dated 1823-99.

Indexes.--A card index, arranged alphabetically by name of passenger, covers the lists for 1875-99. The index to the copies of lists for Atlantic and gulf coast ports exclusive of New York, described below, serves as an index to earlier lists for New Bedford.

New Orleans Lists

The records.--The New Orleans lists are dated 1820-1902, with some lists for January 1903.

Index.--The index to the copies of lists for Atlantic and gulf coast ports exclusive of New York, described below, serves as an index to the original lists for New Orleans to about 1850. There are also a microfilm copy of a card index to passenger arrivals at New Orleans, 1853-99, and a card index to passengers arriving at New Orleans, 1900-January 1903.

Special research aid.--The National Archives Library has five typewritten volumes prepared by the Work Projects Administration of Louisiana entitled "Passenger Lists Taken From Manifests of the Customs Service, Port of New Orleans." These volumes, numbered 1-4 and 6, contain lists for the years 1813-67 and appear to have been copied from cargo manifests and passenger lists now in the National Archives. The alphabetical index in each volume serves as an index, although incomplete, to original passenger lists and abstracts in the National Archives.

New York Lists

The records.--The New York lists are dated 1820-June 17, 1897.

Index.--The index to the copies of lists for New York, described below, serves as an index to part of the original lists for New York.

Philadelphia Lists

The records.--The Philadelphia lists are dated 1820-99. Cargo manifests for 1800-19 and a few of later date containing names of passengers that do not appear on the passenger lists are filed with them.

Indexes.--A card index, arranged alphabetically by name of passenger, contains names on the cargo manifests, 1800-19, names on the passenger lists, 1820-82, and names on some passenger lists, 1883-1906. The index to the copies of lists for Atlantic and gulf coast ports exclusive of New York, described below, serves as a second index to part of the original lists for Philadelphia.

Copies and Abstracts of Lists

The records.--The National Archives has copies and abstracts of passenger lists dated 1820-75. They were made in the offices of the collectors of customs and were usually sent once each quarter to the Secretary of State in accordance with the same act that provided for filing passenger lists with the collectors. Some collectors prepared copies of the individual lists, and others prepared so-called abstracts, which are consolidated lists of names of all passengers who arrived at a given port during the quarter. The practice at a port might vary from time to time.

The collectors at New Orleans also prepared volumes of abstracts that they retained at the port. The National Archives has 23 volumes of these abstracts for the years 1845-75; the separate volumes are dated as follows:

1. Jan. 2, 1845 - Nov. 3, 1845
2. Nov. 3, 1845 - Mar. 15, 1846
3. Mar. 15, 1846 - Jan. 31, 1847
4. Feb. 6, 1847 - Nov. 8, 1847

5. Nov. 8, 1847 - Mar. 16, 1848
6. Mar. 16, 1848 - Nov. 20, 1848
7. Nov. 20, 1848 - Mar. 31, 1849
8. Apr. 2, 1849 - Dec. 31, 1849
9. Jan. 1, 1850 - Dec. 9, 1850
10. Dec. 11, 1850 - Apr. 10, 1851
11. Apr. 10, 1851 - Dec. 29, 1851
12. Jan. 3, 1853 - June 13, 1853
13. June 13, 1853 - Dec. 28, 1853
14. Dec. 29, 1853 - May 25, 1854
15. May 25, 1854 - Dec. 9, 1854
16. Dec. 9, 1854 - Jan. 1, 1855
17. Oct. 1, 1857 - Dec. 31, 1857
18. Apr. 14, 1864 - May 29, 1866
19. June 1, 1866 - Apr. 23, 1867
20. Apr. 25, 1867 - June 1, 1868
21. June 6, 1868 - Oct. 21, 1869
22. Oct. 22, 1869 - July 20, 1870
23. July 3, 1871 - June 30, 1875

Likewise there is one volume of abstracts for the port of Baltimore, 1820, that was retained at the port and later transferred to the National Archives.

The ports or districts for which there are copies or abstracts in the National Archives are shown in the table near the beginning of this chapter.

Indexes. --There are two separate card indexes to the names on the copies and abstracts of passenger lists. One of them contains entries for passengers arriving at the port of New York, 1820-46. The other contains entries for passengers arriving at other Atlantic and gulf coast ports, 1820-74, and includes a few entries for New York passengers. Both indexes are arranged alphabetically by name of passenger. The two indexes also serve as indexes to names appearing on part of the original passenger lists, the first index to names on lists for New York and the second to names on lists for Baltimore, Mobile, New Bedford, New Orleans, and Philadelphia.

Information in the records. --The copies of the passenger lists usually contain the name of the vessel, the name of the port of embarkation, and the name of the port of arrival, and sometimes the name of the master and the date of arrival. The abstracts usually contain the name of the district or port, the quarter year of arrival, and sometimes the name of the port of embarkation. Both copies and abstracts contain the same information for each passenger that is to be found in the original lists except that some of it may be abbreviated. For example, some copies and abstracts show only the initials of the given names of the passengers.

State Department Transcripts of Lists

The records. --There are eight volumes of transcripts of lists for the years 1819-32 that were apparently prepared in the Department of State from the copies or abstracts sent to the Secretary of State by the collectors of customs. Entries in the volumes are arranged by quarter year of arrival, thereunder by name of district or port, thereunder by name of vessel, and thereunder by name of passenger.

Volume 2 of the transcripts is missing, but some of it is reproduced in the printed work described below as a special research aid. The table below shows the quarters of the year with which each volume begins and ends. It should be noted that the entries for some quarters begin in one volume and end in the next. For example, volume 3 ends with the quarter year ending June 30, 1823, and volume 4 begins with the same quarter. Therefore an entry for a passenger arriving between April 1, 1823, and June 30, 1823, might be in either volume.

Volume	Begins with quarter ending	Ends with quarter ending
1	December 31, 1819	September 30, 1820
3	September 30, 1821	June 30, 1823
4	June 30, 1823	September 30, 1824
5	September 30, 1824	September 30, 1825
6	September 30, 1825	September 30, 1826
7	September 30, 1826	March 31, 1827
8	March 31, 1827	June 30, 1827
9	June 30, 1827	December 31, 1832

Indexes.--An index to the entries in volume 1 is mentioned under special research aid below. The indexes to the copies and abstracts of lists described above serve as incomplete indexes to entries in the volumes.

Information in the records.--A typical entry shows the name of the vessel, the quarter year in which it arrived, the name of its master, the name of the district or port of arrival, and, for each passenger, his name, age, sex, and occupation, name of country to which he belonged, and name of country that he intended to inhabit. If his death occurred en route, information about it is given. Errors have been noted in these volumes that are not in the copies or abstracts sent to the Department of State.

Special research aid.--All entries in volume 1 and some entries from the missing volume 2 were printed in Letter from the Secretary of State With a Transcript of the List of Passengers Who Arrived in the United States from the 1st October, 1819, to the 30th September, 1820 (16th Cong., 2d sess., S. Doc. 118, serial 45). The National Archives Library has a typescript index to this volume.

Use of the records.--The volumes are useful because they include transcripts of lists not otherwise known. For example, the information appearing in the abstracts for 1819 and the information about New York arrivals during the second quarter of 1820 are not available elsewhere in records in the National Archives.

RECORD GROUP

The customs passenger lists are in Record Group 36, Records of the Bureau of Customs.

CUSTOMS LISTS OF ALIENS

The National Archives has customs lists of aliens for the ports of Salem and Beverly, Mass., 1798-1800. They were made in accordance with an act of Congress approved June 25, 1798, requiring masters of ships coming into United States ports to file lists of aliens aboard ship with the collectors of customs. Lists for any other ports are not known to be among the records in the National Archives. Although the act provided that copies of the lists should be submitted to the Department of State, the whereabouts of such copies is not known.

Index.--None.

Information in the records.--Lists of aliens contain some or all of the following information: name of vessel, name of its master, date of its arrival, and names of the ports of embarkation and arrival; and for each alien, his name, age, birthplace, name of the country from which he came, name of the nation to which he belonged and owed allegiance, occupation, and personal description.

Printed aid.--The Salem and Beverly lists were transcribed and printed in The New England Historical and Genealogical Register, 106:203-209 (July 1952).

RECORD GROUP

The customs lists of aliens are in Record Group 36, Records of the Bureau of Customs.

IMMIGRATION PASSENGER LISTS

The records.--The National Archives has received from the Immigration and Naturalization Service negative microfilm copies of passenger lists, 1883-1945, maintained by the Service and its predecessors and often referred to as immigration passenger lists or manifests. The lists include the names not only of immigrants but also of American citizens returning from abroad and visitors. The ports for which there are microfilm copies of the lists, and the dates covered, are shown in the table near the beginning of this chapter.

By an act of Congress approved August 3, 1882 (22 Stat. 214), procedures for dealing with the arrival of immigrants were established. Federal officials began to use records made in compliance with State laws and gradually developed forms based on those used by customs officials. Under terms of an act approved March 3, 1891 (26 Stat. 1085), masters of vessels were required to submit certain information about aliens aboard their vessels, and later acts required more detailed information. With the advent of air transportation, similar legislation was passed requiring information on persons entering the country by plane.

Restrictions on the use of records.--Copies of the immigration passenger lists that are less than 50 years old and the related indexes cannot be used. Negative microfilm copies of lists 50 years old or older and the related indexes also cannot be used because of the danger of damaging the film; as positive microfilm prints of these older records are made, the prints can be used.

Indexes.--The National Archives can make available for examination microfilm copies of the following indexes to immigration passenger lists provided all the entries on a roll relate to lists over 50 years old:

Boston, book index, April 1, 1899-September 14, 1940, arranged chronologically by date of vessel arrival, thereunder by class of passenger, and thereunder for the most part alphabetically by the first letter of the surname of the passenger; and a card index, 1902-June 30, 1906, arranged alphabetically.

New York, book index, January 1, 1906-December 31, 1942, arranged chronologically by year, thereunder by vessel line or group of vessel lines, thereunder chronologically by date of vessel arrival, and thereunder alphabetically by the first letter of the surname of the passenger; and a card index, June 16, 1897-June 30, 1902, arranged alphabetically.

Philadelphia, book index, May 14, 1906-June 17, 1926, arranged by vessel line, thereunder chronologically by date of vessel arrival, thereunder, in part, by class of passenger, and thereunder alphabetically by the first letter of the surname of the passenger; and an alphabetic card index, 1800-

1906, to the customs passenger lists, which, although incomplete for the years 1883-1906, also serves as an index to part of the immigration passenger lists.

Portland, Maine, book index, April 1907-April 6, 1930, arranged chronologically by date of vessel arrival and thereunder alphabetically by the first letter of the surname of the passenger.

Providence, book index, December 13, 1911-June 26, 1934, arranged chronologically by date of vessel arrival and thereunder alphabetically by the first letter of the surname of the passenger.

Information in the records.--The microfilm copies of the immigration passenger lists more than 50 years old vary in informational content. The earliest ones, which are for Philadelphia, include reproductions of forms required by Pennsylvania law. They contain the following information: name of master, name of vessel, names of ports of arrival and embarkation, and date of arrival; and for each passenger, his name, place of birth, last legal residence, age, occupation, and sex, and remarks. Forms prescribed by Federal law soon came into use and by 1893 an immigration passenger list included, in addition to the name of the master, the name of the vessel, the names of the ports of arrival and embarkation, and the date of arrival, the following information for each passenger: his name in full, age, sex, marital status, occupation, nationality, last residence, port of arrival in the United States, and final destination in the United States; whether he had been in the United States before and, if so, when and where; and whether he was going to join a relative and, if so, the relative's name, address, and relationship to the passenger. The format of the immigration passenger lists was revised in 1903 to include race; in 1906 to include a personal description and the birthplace; and in 1907 to include the name and address of an alien's nearest relative in the country from which he came.

RECORD GROUP

The immigration passenger lists are in Record Group 85, Records of the Immigration and Naturalization Service.

GENERAL AIDS TO THE USE OF PASSENGER LISTS

Because the indexes to the names on the passenger lists are incomplete and because many of the indexes to the immigration passenger lists are arranged chronologically, it is much easier to find the record of the arrival of a given person if the following information is known: the name of the port of entry, the name of the vessel, and the exact or approximate arrival date. If the name of the port of entry and the approximate arrival date are known, it may be possible to determine the name of the vessel from records of vessel entrances maintained at the ports and now in the National Archives. These volumes show the name of each vessel, the name of its captain, the name of the port of embarkation, and the date of the vessel's arrival. For some ports there are two series of volumes, in one of which the entries are arranged alphabetically by name of vessel and in the other, chronologically. If in addition to the name of the port of entry and the approximate arrival date the port of embarkation is known, it is possible to narrow the search. For example, if a passenger embarked from Stockholm for New York in a year in which 500 passenger vessels arrived in New York, it would be possible to confine the search to the relatively few passenger lists for vessels sailing from Stockholm.

The Morton Allan Directory of European Passenger Steamship Arrivals (New York, Immigration Information Bureau, Inc., 1931) contains information concerning vessels arriving at the ports of New York, 1890-1930, and of Baltimore, Boston, and Philadelphia, 1904-26. It lists by year, name of steamship company, and exact date the names of vessels arriving at these ports for the periods indicated.

Naturalization records may aid in locating the passenger lists of immigrants who later petitioned for naturalization. Some naturalization records show for each petitioner his full name and the date and the name of the port of his arrival in the United States. The 19th century naturalization proceedings for the District of Columbia are in the National Archives. Records of naturalization proceedings in Federal courts outside of the District of Columbia are commonly to be found in records of the district court for the district in which the proceedings took place. If the proceedings were held in a State or local court, the clerk of the court will, as a rule, have the records.

If the name of the court in which an immigrant was naturalized is not known, it may sometimes be learned from lists of voters in the county where he resided. Whether such lists have been preserved may be determined for some counties through inventories of county records prepared by the Work Projects Administration. Inventories for some counties have been printed, and the printed inventories are in the National Archives.

Family records in private possession, such as journals or diaries, may also provide the information that will make an effective search possible.

For some ports there are hundreds of passenger lists for each year, many of them containing hundreds of names each. Therefore, a general search is impractical unless the searcher wishes to spend days or weeks making the search. The number of passengers arriving annually at the principal ports of the United States for several decades appears on a table in Treasury Department, Bureau of Statistics, Arrivals of Alien Passengers and Immigrants in the United States from 1820 to 1892 (Washington, 1893). This table (insofar as it pertains to ports for which there are passenger lists in the National Archives) is reproduced here in order to assist the searcher in determining whether or not it is practical for him to undertake a general search.

Number of Passengers, 1823-55, and Immigrants, 1856-92, Arriving at Certain U. S. Ports

Years Ending	New York, N. Y.	Boston and Charlestown, Mass.	Philadelphia, Pa.	Baltimore, Md.	New Orleans, La.	Charleston, S. C.
Sept. 30, 1823	4,247	672	463	562	1,058	402
1824	4,889	737	1,273	610	1,014	158
1825	7,662	858	1,363	1,365	429	447
1826	6,908	1,170	2,275	1,434	1,100	325
1827	12,602	1,858	3,556	1,706	1,341	341
1828	19,860	1,496	3,500	1,951	1,958	349
1829	14,814	1,595	1,468	1,691	3,044	231
1830	13,748	1,520	1,890	3,943	2,287	152
1831	10,737	1,417	3,808	3,711	3,191	107
Dec. 31, 1832[a]	35,246	3,344	4,747	9,979	4,397	---
1833	39,440	3,240	4,216	4,619	4,785	214
1834	46,053	2,931	4,170	6,913	4,035	89
1835	32,715	3,168	1,705	3,566	3,552	280
1836	58,617	3,258	2,507	6,129	4,966	328
1837	51,676	3,673	4,194	6,632	8,683	393
1838	24,935	2,070	2,159	5,234	7,434	477
1839	47,688	3,046	3,949	6,081	10,306	545
1840	60,609	5,361	4,079	7,271	11,085	224
1841	55,885	8,634	3,016	4,511	10,700	204
1842	74,014	8,021	3,369	5,310	12,922	169
Sept. 30, 1843[b]	38,930	3,654	2,297	2,953	6,055	38
1844	59,762	6,355	4,886	5,006	3,899	330
1845	76,514	10,281	5,767	7,031	15,537	309
1846	98,863	13,998	7,236	9,337	22,148	408
1847	145,830	20,745	14,777	12,018	34,803	164
1848	160,994	22,102	9,824	7,091	19,299	336
1849	213,736	29,490	15,511	8,072	25,209	1,008
Dec. 31, 1850[c]	221,713	31,503	13,713	9,227	51,069	1,617
1851	294,445	25,187	18,556	8,589	52,011	1,811
1852	303,153	21,831	17,959	14,148	32,302	1,517
1853	294,818	25,832	19,211	11,368	43,028	1,069
1854	327,976	27,483	15,032	13,154	51,169	1,133
1855	161,490	17,735	7,581	6,830	20,388	772
1856	140,757	14,353	6,933	6,105	18,758	382

[a]Fifteen months ending December 31, 1832.
[b]Nine months ending September 30, 1843.
[c]Fifteen months ending December 31, 1850.

747-596 O - 64 - 4

Number of Passengers, 1823-55, and Immigrants, 1856-92
Arriving at Certain U. S. Ports--Continued

Years Ending	Galveston, Tex.	Key West, Fla.	Mobile, Ala.	New Bedford, Mass.	New Haven, Conn.	Norfolk and Portsmouth, Va.	Portland and Falmouth, Me.	Providence, R. I.	Savannah, Ga.
Sept. 30, 1823	-----	-----	---	9	69	70	13	27	26
1824	-----	-----	---	---	32	132	55	12	20
1825	-----	-----	---	13	93	92	38	160	23
1826	-----	-----	---	96	58	116	112	23	17
1827	-----	-----	---	12	19	127	27	4	---
1828	-----	-----	---	---	--	96	---	---	---
1829	-----	-----	---	---	31	242	53	29	---
1830	-----	-----	---	---	45	523	122	---	---
1831	-----	-----	---	23	33	552	18	---	---
Dec. 31, 1832[a]	-----	-----	231	76	98	191	34	27	---
1833	-----	-----	---	46	75	187	35	27	---
1834	-----	-----	---	16	65	200	89	64	---
1835	-----	-----	---	27	79	33	33	6	---
1836	-----	49	---	38	49	163	2,027	47	---
1837	-----	275	---	26	42	146	89	90	---
1838	-----	158	---	22	33	32	45	36	---
1839	-----	62	---	16	29	11	56	30	---
1840	-----	38	---	30	49	247	40	19	---
1841	-----	39	---	25	46	25	85	41	---
1842	-----	47	---	22	54	8	696	56	---
Sept. 30, 1843[b]	-----	100	---	13	34	2	-----	22	---
1844	-----	58	---	45	58	10	25	133	---
1845	-----	83	---	51	10	---	122	133	---
1846	354	90	---	30	--	31	123	71	---
1847	3,873	188	---	66	--	660	1,115	55	11
1848	622	79	---	76	--	385	2,638	67	37
1849	439	75	172	31	--	349	2,260	71	209
Dec. 31, 1850[c]	1,306	185	728	156	--	17	2,556	142	371
1851	1,208	81	344	53	--	---	2,424	70	510
1852	2,600	70	299	64	--	---	1,142	36	397
1853	2,081	93	209	64	--	208	517	80	42
1854	3,058	242	191	82	--	12	1,857	61	---
1855	2,048	219	166	201	--	3	321	66	---
1856	1,562	145	66	1	--	12	153	45	---

[a]Fifteen months ending December 31, 1832.

[b]Nine months ending September 30, 1843.

[c]Fifteen months ending December 31, 1850.

Number of Passengers, 1823-55, and Immigrants, 1856-92
Arriving at Certain U. S. Ports--Continued

Years Ending	New York, N. Y.	Boston and Charlestown, Mass.	Philadelphia, Pa.	Baltimore, Md.	New Orleans, La.	Charleston, S. C.
Dec. 31, 1857	188,243	13,331	5,275	8,923	21,299	402
1858	85,848	5,086	2,264	3,690	11,466	384
1859	86,449	8,498	3,311	3,546	8,545	350
1860	111,461	8,807	3,426	6,709	10,663	94
1861	70,063	4,365	1,634	3,725	727	---
1862	78,395	2,356	1,434	2,237	------	---
1863	151,956	7,217	3,688	1,070	------	---
1864	174,434	6,347	4,240	2,917	------	---
1865	190,372	10,007	1,560	4,457	3,572	21
June 30, 1866[d]	120,099	4,534	1,892	3,937	1,856	15
1867	240,030	11,483	2,580	10,035	4,884	190
1868	235,553	12,529	826	9,740	3,772	125
1869	253,754	23,294	1,061	11,202	3,424	331
1870	256,354	37,028	1,016	11,527	4,784	127
1871	206,205	27,024	348	9,956	4,181	29
1872	283,226	26,909	154	15,979	6,005	5
1873	307,334	37,676	1,108	17,897	6,304	52
1874	194,144	24,225	5,649	9,831	4,915	---
1875	130,994	17,645	9,929	6,055	2,132	33
1876	82,373	9,711	7,812	5,093	1,669	---
1877	72,942	7,887	6,154	3,923	1,801	11
1878	72,163	8,756	5,289	3,612	2,449	---
1879	99,224	10,364	8,266	4,713	1,834	---
1880	263,726	34,062	21,727	17,934	2,663	4
1881	400,871	41,018	34,865	40,017	3,284	2
1882	502,171	58,186	36,284	41,739	3,142	5
1883	406,697	48,188	24,808	35,690	1,707	4
1884	354,702	35,036	18,981	35,507	4,093	3
1885	287,223	25,660	22,482	15,928	2,325	---
1886	266,370	25,046	20,822	13,500	1,648	1
1887	376,005	36,209	31,048	36,098	2,031	7
1888	418,423	44,873	37,325	33,297	2,962	---
1889	338,784	35,198	28,100	29,704	3,706	2
1890	364,086	29,813	22,658	27,178	3,878	4
1891	448,403	30,951	26,152	40,694	3,963	2
1892	489,810	32,343	31,102	55,820	3,817	---

[d]Six months.

Number of Passengers, 1823-55, and Immigrants, 1856-92
Arriving at Certain U. S. Ports--Continued

Years Ending	Galveston, Tex.	Key West, Fla.	Mobile, Ala.	New Bedford, Mass.	New Haven, Conn.	Norfolk and Portsmouth, Va.	Portland and Falmouth, Me.	Providence, R. I.	Savannah, Ga.
Dec. 31, 1857	591	145	190	3	--	223	603	148	---
1858	484	312	62	9	--	-----	143	37	---
1859	679	142	284	117	--	-----	137	67	---
1860	1,258	175	259	6	--	-----	1,047	79	---
1861	-----	51	---	1	--	-----	1,211	18	---
1862	-----	125	---	60	--	-----	267	29	---
1863	-----	128	---	128	--	-----	2,791	27	---
1864	-----	199	---	427	--	-----	1,082	16	---
1865	-----	185	---	112	10	-----	3,590	23	15
June 30, 1866[d]	-----	96	---	---	2	-----	3,408	---	---
1867	1,294	187	---	75	7	-----	3,806	28	11
1868	1,845	141	---	15	4	-----	4,319	69	15
1869	709	476	---	76	6	-----	4,026	13	4
1870	1,204	1,009	---	70	2	-----	3,435	8	10
1871	732	684	---	122	4	71	4,219	15	5
1872	763	924	---	186	13	664	5,385	11	14
1873	1,133	1,114	---	160	5	1,190	4,524	133	34
1874	572	1,272	---	179	2	507	2,477	7	3
1875	135	1,279	---	364	5	-----	1,633	---	1
1876	60	983	---	214	10	-----	1,283	---	7
1877	53	963	---	402	6	-----	977	---	---
1878	2	623	---	183	1	-----	27	---	---
1879	18	820	---	841	2	-----	42	1	---
1880	7	996	---	274	9	-----	53	4	---
1881	1,278	1,441	---	501	3	-----	15	3	---
1882	1,351	1,011	---	445	14	-----	2,006	1	---
1883	1,535	690	---	496	20	-----	1,845	5	---
1884	1,958	2,029	---	435	13	-----	1,716	2	1
1885	964	2,289	3	512	16	-----	866	--	---
1886	560	2,427	---	372	20	-----	1,658	--	---
1887	462	4,596	1	500	8	-----	1,076	--	---
1888	79	4,436	---	825	2	-----	160	--	---
1889	40	4,545	---	673	7	-----	481	--	---
1890	22	2,482	---	947	6	-----	531	1	---
1891	65	3,301	---	866	--	-----	379	--	3
1892	26	1,138	1	678	--	1	1,436	48	7

[d] Six months.

For information about publications concerning early passenger lists, consult the bibliography by A. Harold Lancour, "Passenger Lists of Ships Coming to North America 1607-1825," which comprises an issue of the Bulletin of the New York Public Library, (vol. 41, No. 5, 1937).

The National Archives Library has 6 typed leaflets containing the names of persons who emigrated in 1833-35 chiefly to the United States and Canada from various parishes in County Londonderry, Ireland. They were prepared by the Public Record Office of Northern Ireland from Irish records.

The Manuscript Division, Library of Congress, Washington 25, D. C., has microfilm copies of passenger lists of emigrants from Hamburg, Germany, 1850-73, and related indexes. The lists are described in Marion Dexter Learned, Guide to the Manuscript Materials Relating to American History in the German State Archives, p. 274 (Washington, 1912).

III. UNITED STATES MILITARY RECORDS

The National Archives has United States military records dated 1775-1912, with a few as late as 1917 and records of burials to 1939. They are incomplete because fires in Washington, D. C., on November 8, 1800, and August 24, 1814, destroyed many Revolutionary War and other records. The extant records include military service records of the Regular Army, 1784-1917, but chiefly 1800-1912; military records of the Revolutionary War, 1775-83; military service records of volunteer organizations of the War of 1812, Mexican War, Civil War, Spanish-American War, and other periods of military operations, 1784-1903; miscellaneous military records, 1784-1815; Civil War draft records, 1863-65; burial records of soldiers, 1775-1939; and records of births, marriages, and civilian deaths at army posts, 1884-1912.

MILITARY SERVICE RECORDS OF THE REGULAR ARMY

The military service records of the Regular Army are dated chiefly 1800-1912 with some as late as June 1917. Earlier records, which are fragmentary, begin in 1784, and concern in part the predecessor Army of the Congress of the Confederation. The records relate to commissioned officers, cadets of the United States Military Academy, and enlisted men.

Records Relating to Commissioned Officers

The records relating to commissioned officers are dated chiefly 1805-June 1917. They include documents relating to individual officers in correspondence files, muster rolls, registers of commissions, card abstracts relating to staff officers of the Civil War, and military histories of officers.

Documents Relating to Individual Officers in Correspondence Files

The records.--Documents known as personal papers or one-name papers, filed among the correspondence, are regarded as the basic service records for officers of the Regular Army. The National Archives has such records for the period 1805-June 1917. They include letters of acceptance of commission, oaths of office, and requests for reassignment, and, in some cases, reports and copies of summaries of service records prepared in answer to inquiries. These personal papers form parts of large correspondence series of The Adjutant General's Office. Except for some of the earlier records, the records for each officer are consolidated into a single file that is identified by an appropriate symbol. The personal papers fall into the following chronological groups:

1805-62. Personal papers for these years are included in the series of letters received by the Adjutant General's Office. For the period 1805-

21 this series is arranged by year, thereunder alphabetically by surname of writer. For the period 1821-62, the series is arranged by year, thereunder by initial letter of surname of writer, thereunder by file number. The registers of letters received, which serve as keys for the period 1814-62, contain cross references to the consolidated files for each officer.

1863-June 1894. The personal papers are included in the series of letters received (beginning in 1889 letters received and sent) of the Appointment, Commission and Personal Branch. Bound registers of letters received and indexes to letters received identify documents by file number.

July 1894-June 1917. The personal papers are included in the document file of The Adjutant General's Office, 1890-1917. A special card index identifies by name and file number the consolidated file relating to each officer.

Information in the records.--These documents include such information as the name, rank, military organization, and station of each officer, the name of the State from which he was appointed, the date of acceptance of his commission, the date and nature of his separation from the service, and a summary statement of advances in his rank and assignments. Documents relating to officers who served after 1890 include such additional information as the date and place of the officer's birth, the place of his residence, the number of his minor children, and the name, address, and relationship of his nearest relative.

Muster Rolls

The records.--The muster rolls, dated 1784-1912, are described below under records relating to enlisted men. They are useful for the period 1784-1804, before the date of the beginning of the basic correspondence files; or, for a later period, when needed to fill out minor details of an officer's career.

Registers of Commissions

The records.--Dated 1792-1899, the registers include registers of army commissions, 1792-1812, registers of army commissions, 1801-95, in 24 volumes, and registers of brevet commissions, 1825-99, in 6 volumes. The registers show such information as the name of the officer, the date of his commission, his rank, and, for brevet commissions, the reason for the commission. A name index is in each volume.

Card Abstracts Relating to Staff Officers, Civil War

The records.--The compiled military service records of Civil War staff officers relate to volunteer officers as well as Regular Army officers. They are described below under "Military service records of volunteer organizations, records of the Civil War."

Military Histories of Officers

The records.--Military histories of some Regular Army and volunteer officers, chiefly those having Civil War service, were prepared between 1875 and 1890 and were bound in two volumes. They contain citations to the consolidated files upon which they were based. Each volume contains an index.

Research aids.--For the name and organization of each Regular Army officer, 1789-1903, see Francis B. Heitman, Historical Register and Dictionary of the United States Army, vol. 1, p. 147-1069 (Washington, 1903). For officers who were graduates of the U. S. Military Academy, see also the section below.

Records Relating to Cadets of the United States Military Academy

The records.--The application papers of cadets, 1805-1904, consist of letters of application, letters of recommendation, and statements of consent signed by parents or guardians. They are arranged in chronological groups as follows:

1805-15, 1830-32. The letters relating to applicants are arranged in rough chronological order and are not indexed.

1814-66. The papers relating to each applicant are filed together and are arranged by year of application, thereunder by file number. There is a one-volume index.

1867-1904. The application papers are interfiled in the series of correspondence relating to the Military Academy. Except for 1867-69, when the papers are arranged by year and thereunder by initial letter of writer's name, the papers relating to each applicant are filed together and are arranged by year and thereunder numerically. The file numbers of the application papers for the period 1867-94 are shown in bound Military Academy registers, in which the entries are arranged by year, thereunder by name of State, and thereunder by Congressional district. Another register, 1866-94, arranged by initial letter of surname, shows the date of appointment, the name of the State, and the number of the Congressional district of each candidate for appointment. An alphabetical card register of cadet warrants, 1895-1917, identifies later cadets by name and date of appointment.

Information in the records.--The papers show the name, age, and place of residence of each candidate and such additional information as the name of a parent or guardian, the name of the school attended, and data on family background.

Research aid.--See George W. Cullum, Biographical Register of the Officers and Graduates of the United States Military Academy at West Point, (3d ed. rev., Boston and New York, 1891-1930).

Records Relating to Enlisted Men

Military service records relating to enlisted men of the Regular Army include muster rolls, enlistment papers, registers of enlistments, and documents relating to individual men.

Muster Rolls

The records.--The muster rolls, 1784-October 31, 1912, are lists of troops present or accounted for on the dates of musters. They constitute the basic evidence of military service. They are arranged by periods as follows:

1784-92. Incomplete. Intermixed with the largely unarranged "Post-Revolutionary War Papers".

1791-95. For Wayne's War. Arranged by name of sublegion of the Legion of the United States.

1795-1821. Arranged in general by branch of service such as cavalry, artillery, or infantry, thereunder by number of regiment, thereunder chronologically.

1821-October 31, 1912. Arranged by branch of service, thereunder by number of regiment, thereunder by company or unit, thereunder chronologically.

Information in the records.--A muster roll shows the name of each soldier, the date and place of the muster, the designation of the military unit, the name of the commanding officer, and, when appropriate, remarks concerning the soldier's whereabouts or health.

Use of the muster rolls.--Since the muster rolls are not indexed and generally contain less information than the enlistment or other records, they are useful primarily when other records are lacking or when it is desired to fill out minor details of a soldier's career.

Enlistment Papers

The records.--The enlistment papers are dated chiefly 1800-October 31, 1912, with a few as early as 1792. Those dated 1792-1820 are arranged by the initial letter of the surname; those dated 1821-July 14, 1894, are for the most part arranged alphabetically by name of enlisted man; those dated July 15, 1894-October 31, 1912, are in jackets, which are arranged alphabetically by name of enlisted man. The jackets include also personal or one-name papers, such as hospital corps cards, description and assignment cards, and final statements or reports of death and burial. The enlistment papers relating to Indian scouts, 1866-1914, are separately filed and indexed in four volumes.

Information in the records.--An enlistment paper normally shows the name of the enlisted man; his place of birth; age; occupation; the date and place of his enlistment or reenlistment; the period for which he enlisted; his personal description; and his military organization. Enlistment papers made out after July 15, 1894, show the name and address of the person to be notified in case of emergency and his relationship to the enlisted man; and if the enlisted man is a minor, the name of his parent or guardian. A death report, one of the personal papers filed in the jacket with the enlistment papers, shows the man's name, rank, the date and place of his death, and sometimes the place of his burial.

Registers of Enlistments

The records.--The registers of enlistments, 1798-1914, with some entries as early as 1793, are in about 140 large volumes. They have also been microfilmed. They summarize the information chiefly in the enlistment papers but also, for the years 1798-1821, in the muster rolls, inspection returns, and some other records. For the most part they are arranged by date of enlistment in chronological groups as follows:

1793-May 15, 1815. Each of 26 registers contains entries for surnames beginning with 1 or more letters of the alphabet. There is some overlapping. The following table shows the initial letter or letters of the surnames included in each volume:

1	A	8	D	15	L	22	S
2	B	9	F	16	M	23	S, T
3	B	10	G	17	M	24	T, U, V, W
4	B	11	H	18	M, N, O	25	W
5	C	12	H	19	P	26	W, Y, Z
6	C	13	I, J	20	Q, R		
7	D, E, H	14	K, L	21	R, S		

Entries under each letter of the alphabet are sometimes arranged alphabetically or alphabetically to the first letter of the given name.

May 17, 1815-June 30, 1821. Nine registers contain entries that are grouped alphabetically according to the initial letters of the surnames of the enlisted men and thereunder according to the initial letters of their given names. The following table shows the initial letters of the surnames included in each volume:

27	A, B, C, D	30	G, H	33	N, O, P, Q, R
28	B	31	I, J, K	34	S, T
29	D, E, F	32	L, M	35	U, V, W, Y, Z

July 1, 1821-October 31, 1914. There is usually a register for each period of a year or more. Entries are arranged alphabetically by the initial letter of the surname, and thereunder alphabetically by the initial letter of the given name.

Each entry in a register relates to a single enlistment and is recorded on one line extending across two facing pages.

Information in the records.--The entries vary in detail, some entries up to May 15, 1815, being fragmentary. A full entry shows the name of the enlisted man; the date, place, and period of his enlistment or reenlistment; the name of the town, county, or State where he was born; his occupation and personal description; the designation of his regiment and company; and the date and nature of his separation from the service.

Use of the records.--For the period 1792-June 30, 1821, the registers of enlistments are usually the most satisfactory records to use to identify the service of an enlisted man.

Documents Relating to Individual Men

The records.--These documents, often known as personal papers, are dated 1812-1912 and include certificates of disability, final statement papers, and burial records. There are separate series of certificates of disability, 1812-99, and final statements, 1862-99. Some personal papers, 1861-65, are arranged alphabetically by name of enlisted man. Many personal papers, July 15, 1894-October 31, 1912, are filed in the jackets for enlisted men described above under "enlistment papers." Other personal papers are generally unarranged. Copies of the certificates of disability are normally filed in the pension application files.

RECORD GROUP

The military service records of the Regular Army are in Record Group 94, Records of The Adjutant General's Office.

MILITARY RECORDS OF THE REVOLUTIONARY WAR

The military records of the Revolutionary War are dated 1775-83 but some are interfiled with documents of later dates. They relate to the troops of the Continental Army, some of the State troops, and a few of the State militia.

They are divided into two groups: records collected or compiled by the Adjutant General's Office, and pay records of the Treasury Department.

Records Collected or Compiled by the Adjutant General's Office

The records collected by the Adjutant General's Office were collected chiefly between 1873 and 1913 to replace original records destroyed by fire. They were obtained from the War, State, Treasury, and Interior Departments and from private sources. They include Army returns from the papers of George Washington; the papers of Timothy Pickering, member of the Board of War, Adjutant General, and Quartermaster General; the papers of Samuel Hodgdon, Commisary General of Military Stores; and copies of Virginia and other State records. These records were arbitrarily divided into two collections: muster rolls, pay rolls, and related unbound records; and "books," "manuscripts," and "photostats." The basic military service records of the National Government for the Revolutionary War, described below, were compiled by the Adjutant General's Office from the former of these collections.

Compiled Military Service Records

The records.--These records consist of cards, about 3 1/2" x 8" in size, on which has been abstracted the information in the muster rolls, pay rolls, and related records referred to above. Each card contains all the information about one soldier that is on a single document, and all the cards relating to the same soldier are filed together in one jacket-envelope. The cards were so carefully prepared that the records on which they are based are rarely consulted except to ascertain the names of fellow soldiers.

The jacket-envelopes are divided into three main groups: (1) those for the Continental Army, which are arranged by name of organization and thereunder alphabetically by name of soldier; (2) those for State troops, which are arranged by name of State, thereunder by name of organization, and thereunder alphabetically by name of soldier; and (3) others, which are filed under the headings Commissary of Military Stores Department, naval personnel, and miscellaneous, and thereunder alphabetically by name of serviceman.

Indexes to the compiled military service records.--The indexes, on cards approximately 3 1/2" x 8", include a master name index, a name index for Continental troops, and a name index for each State and for each non-State organization or unit. The master name index and the index for North Carolina have been microfilmed. Indexes for other States are being microfilmed.

Information in the records.--The records show such information as the name, rank, and military organization of the soldier; if available, the name of the State from which he served; the date that his name appears on one or more rolls; sometimes the date or dates and period of his enlistment or the date of his appointment; and rarely the date of his separation from the service.

Research aids.--Many publications contain information identifying Revolutionary War soldiers and showing their service. Some of these publications show the name and military organization of each soldier named and are based in whole or in part on State service records or State and National service records. They often supply identifying information that will make possible effective searches in the records in the National Archives, or they supplement the incomplete records in the National Archives.

The following publication relates to officers: Francis B. Heitman, Historical Register of Officers of the Continental Army During the War of the Revolution, April 1775 to December 1783 (new rev. and enl. ed. Washington, 1914).

Following is a select list of publications arranged by name of State that show the names and as a rule the military organizations of many soldiers who served:

Connecticut, Adjutant-General's Office, Record of Service of Connecticut Men in the I.-War of the Revolution. II.-War of 1812. III.-Mexican War (Hartford, 1889). Connecticut Historical Society, Collections of the Connecticut Historical Society, vols. 8 and 12 (Hartford, 1901 and 1909).

Delaware Public Archives Commission, Delaware Archives, vols. 1-3 (Wilmington, 1911-19).

Georgia, Department of Archives and History, Georgia's Roster of the Revolution, p. 374-435 (Atlanta, 1920).

Maryland Historical Society, Archives of Maryland, vol. 18 (Baltimore, 1900).

Massachusetts, Secretary of the Commonwealth, Massachusetts Soldiers and Sailors of the Revolutionary War (Boston, 1896-1908). This publication includes Maine.

Isaac Weare Hammond, Rolls of the Soldiers in the Revolutionary War (Concord, 1885-89). Title varies. (In New Hampshire, Provincial and State Papers, vols. 14-17). This publication pertains to New Hampshire.

New Jersey, Adjutant-General's Office, Official Register of the Officers and Men of New Jersey in the Revolutionary War (Trenton, 1872). For index, see Index of the Official Register of the Officers and Men of New Jersey in the Revolutionary War Prepared by the New Jersey Historical Records Survey Program (Newark, 1941).

New York (State) University, Documents Relating to the Colonial History of the State of New York, vol. 15 (Albany, 1887).

New York, Comptroller's Office, New York in the Revolution as County and State (1898 ed. or vol. 1 of 1904 ed.)

North Carolina, The State Records of North Carolina, vol. 16 (Goldsboro, 1899). Consult master index at end of series.

Pennsylvania Archives, 2d series, vols. 10, 11, 13-15; 3d series, vol. 23; 5th series, vols. 1-8; 6th series, vols. 1-2. See the general indexes.

Vermont, Rolls of the Soldiers in the Revolutionary War (Rutland, 1904).

Gwathmey, John H., Historical Register of Virginians in the Revolution; Soldiers, Sailors, Marines (Richmond, 1938).

Virginia, State Library, Department of Archives and History, List of Revolutionary Soldiers of Virginia (Richmond, 1912, 1913).

A list by name of State that identifies some publications not named here is in Gilbert H. Doane, Searching for Your Ancestors, appendix D (2d ed., Minneapolis, 1948).

A list of French participants in the Revolutionary War, based upon French records and published in Paris, was republished and indexed by the United States Government under the title Les Combattants français de la Guerre Américaine, 1778-1783, as Senate Document 77 of the 58th Congress, 2d session (serial 4595). This list appears to relate chiefly to men who returned to France. It is not complete.

For a list of medical men see Louis Caspar Duncan, Medical Men in the American Revolution, 1775-1783, p. 379-414 (Carlisle Barracks, Pa., 1931).

Among the records is a catalog that identifies by name the Revolutionary War organizations.

"Books," "Manuscripts," and "Photostats"

The records.--The books, manuscripts, and photostats relate to soldiers, wagonmasters, officials of the Continental Congress, and others. They are dated chiefly 1775-83, but some documents include entries dated as late as 1798.

The "books" include orderly books, rosters of soldiers, oaths of allegiance of officers of the Continental Army and officials of the Continental Congress, and accounts of receipts and disbursements. They are numbered from 1 to 197, including 136 1/2 and 147 1/2; and each page of each book is numbered consecutively.

The "manuscripts" are chiefly unbound documents such as accounts, receipts, enlistment papers, and correspondence. They are numbered consecutively.

The "photostats" are copies of records in the custody of public and private institutions and of individuals in Virginia, North Carolina, and Massachusetts made in accordance with an act of Congress approved March 2, 1913 (37 Stat. 723). They include correspondence of the State Boards of War, minutes of the boards, and, for Virginia, county court records. For identification of the records copied, including the names of the Virginia counties from which records were copied, consult H. C. Clark, "Report on Publication of Revolutionary Military Records," in Annual Report of the American Historical Association for the Year 1915, p. 193-199. The photostats for Virginia and some of those for Massachusetts are numbered.

Index to the records.--A master name index on cards approximately 3 1/2" x 8", identifies entries in the books, the manuscripts, the numbered photostats for Massachusetts, and some of the photostats for Virginia. There is a separate and more nearly complete card index to the photostats for Virginia.

Information in the records.--Since the documents vary greatly, the information they contain also varies greatly. An indexed document includes the name of a person and usually evidence of his participation in the Revolutionary War; and, if he is a soldier, identification of his military organization.

Research aids.--Volume 97 of the "books," the daybook of Peter Anspach, has been reproduced in facsimile as Day Book of Peter Anspach, Paymaster to the Quartermaster General's Department September 10, 1781 to May 17, 1782 with a foreword and index by Nellie P. Waldenmaier (Washington, 1941). Volumes 165-168 of the "books," oaths of allegiance and fidelity, together with oaths in the Papers of Continental Congress (RG 11) have been abstracted, indexed, and printed in Nellie P. Waldenmaier, Some of the Earliest Oaths of Allegiance to the United States of America (Lancaster, Pa., 1944).

Pay Records of the Treasury Department

The records.--The Treasury Department records include the company record of the 1st Pennsylvania Line; the company book of Capt. Aaron Ogden, 1st Regiment of Jersey; and Pierce's register of certificates of indebtedness.

Company Record of the 1st Pennsylvania Line

This volume, dated March 1779-August 1780, includes the pay roll and muster roll and is not indexed.

Company Book of Capt. Aaron Ogden, 1st Regiment of Jersey

This volume, dated February 1782-March 1783, includes copies of size rolls, muster rolls, and returns. The size roll shows the name, age, personal description, trade, town, county, and State of birth, place of residence, and date of enlistment of each soldier. The volume is not indexed.

Pierce's Register of Certificates of Indebtedness

Annotated copies of the printed Register of the Certificates Issued by John Pierce, Esquire, Paymaster General, and Commissioner of the Army Accounts, for the United States (New York, Francis Childs, 1786) are among the records of the Bureau of the Public Debt in the National Archives. They name officers and men of the Continental Army (except for South Carolinians) to whom certificates of indebtedness were issued between 1783 and 1787 under the Continental Congress resolution of July 4, 1783, empowering the Paymaster "to settle and finally adjust all accounts whatsoever, between the United States and the officers and soldiers of the American army." An alphabetized reprint of the Register, showing the number of the certificate, to whom issued, and the amount, was published in Daughters of the American Revolution, Seventeenth Report, 1913-14, p. 149-712 (63d Cong., 3d sess., S. Doc. 988; serial 6777).

RECORD GROUPS

The records collected by the Adjutant General's Office are in Record Group 93, War Department Collection of Revolutionary War Records; the pay records of the Treasury Department are in Record Group 53, Records of the Bureau of the Public Debt.

MILITARY SERVICE RECORDS OF VOLUNTEER ORGANIZATIONS

The military service records of volunteer organizations in the National Archives, in addition to the Revolutionary War records described above, relate to service in the War of 1812, Mexican War, Civil War, and Spanish-American War and to some other service performed between the years 1784 and 1865 and the years 1898 and 1903. The records relate to volunteer officers and men and to men who were drafted. They include compiled military service records and documents relating to individuals in correspondence files.

Compiled Military Service Records

The compiled military service records consist of cards, about 3 1/2" x 8", on which has been abstracted information in muster rolls and occasionally in other documents, such as returns, pay vouchers, inspection reports, hospital rolls, and lists of deserters. Each card contains all the information about one soldier that is on a single document, and all the cards relating to the same soldier are filed together in one jacket-envelope. The cards were so carefully prepared that the records on which they are based are rarely consulted except to ascertain the name of fellow soldiers. Filed in the jacket-envelopes with the cards are also originals of papers relating solely to the particular soldiers.

The compiled military service records of volunteer organizations are arranged as follows: records of the Post-Revolutionary War period, records of the War of 1812, records of Indian Wars and related wars, records of the Mexican War, records of the Civil War, records of the Spanish-American War, and records of the Philippine Insurrection.

Records of the Post-Revolutionary War Period

The records.--The compiled military service records of the Post-Revolutionary War period are dated 1784-1811 and consist of card abstracts. The jacket-envelopes in which the cards are filed are arranged alphabetically by name of State, thereunder alphabetically by name of organization, thereunder alphabetically by name of soldier; or by name of organization such as the First and Second Regiments of United States Levies, and thereunder alphabetically by name of soldier.

Indexes to the records.--The indexes include a master name index, an index for each State or group of State organizations, and an index for each non-State organization.

Information in the records.--The records relating to a soldier normally show his name, rank, and military organization; the dates he was mustered in and out; and, where available, the name of the State from which he served.

Records of the War of 1812

The records.--The compiled military service records of the War of 1812 are dated 1812-15 and consist chiefly of card abstracts, with a few subsistence and pay accounts for individual officers. The jacket-envelopes in which they are filed are arranged by name of State, thereunder by name of military organization, and thereunder alphabetically by name of soldier; or by name of non-State organization such as U. S. Volunteer Organizations, Indian Regiments, Prisoners of War, Spies, and Quartermaster Department, and thereunder alphabetically by name of soldier. Since payrolls known as receipts for pay were not abstracted on cards, it is sometimes necessary to consult them to complete a soldier's record.

Indexes to the records.--The indexes include a master name index, an index for each State, and an index for each non-State organization. The indexes for Louisiana and North Carolina have been microfilmed.

Information in the records.--The records relating to a soldier normally show his name, rank, and military organization; the dates he was mustered in and out; and, if he served in a State organization, the name of the State from which he served.

Research aids.--The indexed and published State rosters, based largely on State records, include:

Connecticut, Adjutant-General's Office, Record of Service of Connecticut Men in the I.-War of the Revolution. II.-War of 1812. III.-Mexican War (Hartford, 1889).

Delaware Public Archives Commission, Delaware Archives, vols. 4, 5 (Wilmington, 1916).

Louis Henry Dielman, "Maryland Roster, War of 1812," in William Matthew Marine, The British Invasion of Maryland 1812-1815 p. 195-495 (Baltimore, 1913).

Massachusetts, Adjutant General's Office, Records of the Massachusetts Volunteer Militia . . . War of 1812-14 (Boston, 1913). This publication includes Maine.

New Jersey, Adjutant General Office, Records of Officers and Men of New Jersey in Wars 1791-1815 (Trenton, 1909).

Pennsylvania Archives, 2d series, vol. 12; 6th series, vols. 7, 8, 9.

Vermont, Adjutant and Inspector General's Office, Roster of Soldiers in the War of 1812-14 (St. Albans, 1933).

Records of the Indian Wars and Related Wars

The records.--The compiled military service records of the Indian Wars and related wars are dated 1817-58. They concern in part service in the Florida War, the Seminole War, the Black Hawk War, the Creek

War, the Cherokee War, and the Sac and Fox War. Related to these records are the compiled military service records of the Utah Expedition, 1857-58, and the Patriot War, 1838-39.

Indexes to the records.--The indexes include a master name index for the Indian Wars and the Utah Expedition; an index by name of State for the Indian Wars and the Utah Expedition; and two indexes for the Patriot War, one for the Michigan militia, the other for the New York militia. Indexes for Alabama, Louisiana, and North Carolina have been microfilmed.

Information in the records.--The records in a jacket-envelope usually show the name, rank, and military organization of the soldier and the dates he was mustered in and out.

Related information.--For information about Federal troops that served against the Indians before 1817 and after 1858, consult the section on "Military Service Records of the Regular Army."

Records of the Mexican War

The records.--The compiled military service records of the Mexican War are dated 1846-48. They consist chiefly of card abstracts, with only occasional documents relating to individuals. The jacket-envelopes in which the cards are filed are arranged alphabetically by name of State, thereunder by name of military organization, thereunder alphabetically by name of soldier.

Index to the records.--The single master name index is on cards.

Information in the records.--The documents in a jacket-envelope usually show the name, rank, and organization of a soldier, the name of his State, the dates and places he was mustered in and out, and sometimes his age.

Research aids.--For an alphabetical list of volunteer officers in the Mexican War showing rank and organization, consult Francis B. Heitman, Historical Register and Dictionary of the United States Army, vol. 2, p. 43-73 (Washington, 1903).

Related Materials.--With the service jacket-envelopes for each organization are "record of events" jacket-envelopes containing cards showing the military history of the organization.

Records of the Civil War

The records.--The compiled military service records of the Union forces of the Civil War, dated 1861-65, consist of card abstracts and documents relating to individual soldiers, such as voluntary enlistment papers, prisoner-of-war papers, hospital bed cards, and death reports. The cards and sometimes the documents relating to one soldier are filed in a jacket-envelope. The jacket-envelopes for men in State organizations are arranged by name of State; thereunder by arm of service such as cavalry, artillery, or infantry; thereunder numerically by regiment; thereunder alphabetically by name of soldier. The jacket-envelopes for men in other organizations such as the U. S. Sharp Shooters are arranged similarly. Many of the documents relating to individual soldiers in State organizations are not filed in the jacket-envelopes with the related card abstracts but are filed separately in alphabetical order at the end of the file for the State. Some jacket-envelopes include cross-references to the names on the regimental papers that are filed with the muster rolls.

In addition to these basic files there is a separate file of card abstracts pertaining to both volunteer and Regular Army staff officers, which is arranged alphabetically by name of officer.

747-596 O - 64 - 5

Index to the records.--The indexes to the basic files include a separate name index for each State organization and for each non-State organization. The non-State organizations are U. S. Sharp Shooters; U. S. Signal Corps; U. S. Volunteers; Confederate Prisoners of War who enlisted in the United States service; Capt. Turner's Company of Volunteer Prisoners; Veteran Reserve Corps; Brigade Bands; Departmental Corps; Indian Home Guards; and enlisted men from the U. S. Army transferred in February 1862 to the Mississippi Flotilla gunboats Baron de Kalb, Benton, Carondelet, Cincinnati, General Bragg, Judge Torrence, Louisville, Pittsburg, and Conestoga; Pioneer Brigades (Army of the Cumberland); Varner's Battalion of Infantry; and U. S. Colored Troops. Indexes to the service records for Union soldiers from Florida and the Territory of New Mexico have been microfilmed.

Microfilms have been made for indexes to the service records for Union soldiers from the Territory of New Mexico, the Border States of Kentucky, Maryland, and Missouri, and all the Confederate States except South Carolina and for Confederate soldiers from the Territory of Arizona, the Border States of Kentucky, Maryland, and Missouri, and all the Confederate States.

Information in the records.--The records in a jacket-envelope show such information as the name, rank, and military organization of a soldier, the name of his State, the dates and places he was mustered in and out, the date of a change in rank, and the date, place, and nature of his discharge. For some soldiers there is a voluntary enlistment paper or an abstract that shows his age, the town or county of his birth, his occupation, and a personal description. If the soldier was hospitalized, a bed card shows his age, nativity, evidence of whether or not he was married, his place of residence, and the date and occasion of his being wounded. If he died in service, a casualty sheet shows the date and place of his death.

Research aids.--The name and organization of each volunteer officer can be obtained from U. S. Adjutant General's Office, Official Army Register of the Volunteer Force of the United States Army for the Years 1861, '62, '63, '64, '65 (Washington, 1865, 1867). The volumes contain rosters of the officers in each regiment at the time of mustering out, showing the name, rank, and date of appointment of each. They also contain the names of other officers who were at some time in the organization, showing their rank and the date of a change in status, such as the date they resigned, were promoted, or died. There is a personal name index in each volume. Each volume, or part, is devoted to a geographic area, as follows: part I, New England; part II, New York and New Jersey; part III, Pennsylvania, Delaware, Maryland, and the District of Columbia; part IV, West Virginia, Virginia, North Carolina, South Carolina, Georgia, Florida, Alabama, Mississippi, Louisiana, Texas, Arkansas, Tennessee, and Kentucky; part V, Ohio and Michigan; part VI, Indiana and Illinois; part VII, Missouri, Wisconsin, Iowa, Minnesota, California, Kansas, Oregon, and Nevada; and part VIII, Territorial Troops and United States Troops.

Some States published rosters of their troops that were based chiefly or wholly on State records. The indexed rosters are nevertheless useful in searching Federal records. Following is a select list of indexed rosters:

Connecticut, Adjutant-General's Office, Record of Service of Connecticut Men in the Army and Navy of the United States During the War of the Rebellion (Hartford, 1889).

Massachusetts, Adjutant-General's Office, Massachusetts Soldiers, Sailors, and Marines in the Civil War. . . (Norwood, 1931-35). Also one volume Index to Army Records (Boston, 1937). Names of navy men and marines are in vols. 7 and 8 in alphabetical sequences.

Michigan, Adjutant General's Department, Alphabetical General Index to Public Library Sets of 85,271 Names of Michigan Soldiers and Sailors Individual Records (Lansing, 1915).

Minnesota Historical Society, Minnesotans in the Civil and Indian Wars, an Index to the Rosters in Minnesota in the Civil and Indian Wars, 1861-1865 (St. Paul, 1936. Typescript.)

New Hampshire, Adjutant General's Office, Revised Registers of the Soldiers and Sailors of New Hampshire in the War of the Rebellion 1861-1866 (Concord, 1895).

New Jersey, Adjutant-General's Office, Record of Officers and Men of New Jersey in the Civil War, 1861-1865 (Trenton, 1876).

Phisterer, Frederick, comp., New York in the War of the Rebellion, 1861 to 1865 (3d ed., Albany, 1912).

Rhode Island, Adjutant General's Office, Annual Report of the Adjutant General of Rhode Island and Providence Plantations for the Year 1865 (rev., Providence, 1893-95).

Vermont, Adjutant General's Office, Revised Roster of Vermont Volunteers and Lists of Vermonters Who Served in the Army and Navy of the United States During the War of the Rebellion, 1861-66 (Montpelier, 1892).

Wisconsin, Adjutant-General's Office, Wisconsin Volunteers, War of the Rebellion, 1861-1865, Arranged Alphabetically (Madison, 1914).

Use of the records.--In many cases it is difficult to locate the records relating to a soldier unless his military organization is known. Sometimes there were many persons of the same name serving from the same State. Moreover, some soldiers were assigned to non-State organizations such as the U.S. Volunteers, and the State indexes do not locate records pertaining to these soldiers. Some soldiers were mustered in under a spelling of the surname that varies from one used in later life, a frequent occurrence with Pennsylvanians of German ancestry and with soldiers of foreign birth. For such soldiers corresponding pension application files can often be located, and these files identify the respective organizations.

The soldiers of some Missouri organizations that fought against the Confederacy were not in the military service of the United States. These organizations are identified in War Department, Record and Pension Office, Organization and Status of Missouri Troops (Union and Confederate) in Service During the Civil War, p. 227-236 (Washington, 1902. Also published as 57th Cong., 1st sess., S. Doc. 412, serial 4247.) For information about these soldiers, address the Adjutant-General of the State of Missouri, Jefferson City, Mo.

Related information.--The military service records do not normally indicate the battles and engagements in which a soldier participated. They show the period that he was on duty with his regiment, however, and the battles, engagements, and other military activities of his regiment for that period can be ascertained from Frederick H. Dyer, A Compendium of the War of the Rebellion, vol. 3 (New York, 1959).

For alternate names by which military organizations were known, see Adjutant General's Office, List of Synonyms of Organizations in the Volunteer Service of the United States During the years 1861, '62, '63, '64, and '65 (Washington, 1885).

For publications relating to State participation, see War Department, Library, Bibliography of State Participation in the Civil War 1861-1866 (3d ed., Washington, 1913).

Records of the Spanish-American War (and the Puerto Rico Regiment)

The records.--The compiled military service records of the Spanish-American War are dated 1898-99, and of the Puerto Rico Regiment of U. S. Volunteers, 1899-1901. The documents relating to individual soldiers normally include the voluntary enlistment record. The jacket-envelopes and their contents for the Spanish-American War are alphabetically arranged by name of State, thereunder by name of military organization, thereunder alphabetically by name of soldier; or by name of non-State organization, and thereunder alphabetically by name of soldier. The records of the Puerto Rico Regiment are arranged alphabetically by name of soldier.

Indexes to the records.--The indexes include a master name index, an index for each State's volunteer organization, and an index for each U. S. volunteer organization. The index for Louisiana and North Carolina have been microfilmed.

Information in the records.--The records in a jacket-envelope show such information as the name, rank, and military organization of each soldier; the dates and places that he was mustered in and out; his place of birth; his place of residence; his occupation; and, if single, the name and address of a parent or guardian.

Research aid.--For the name, rank, and military organization of each officer who served in volunteer organizations during the Spanish-American War and the Philippine Insurrection see Francis B. Heitman, Historical Register and Dictionary of the United States Army, vol. 2, p. 185-272 (Washington, 1903). This alphabetically arranged list is followed by a list of contract surgeons. For lists with more detailed information about each officer, see Adjutant General's Office, Official Register of Officers of Volunteers in the Service of the United States Organized Under the Act of March 2, 1899 (Washington, 1900).

Records of the Philippine Insurrection

The records.--The compiled military service records of the Philippine Insurrection are dated 1899-1903. The jacket-envelopes are arranged by arm of service, thereunder numerically by regiment, and thereunder alphabetically by surname of soldier.

Indexes to the records.--There is a single name index.

Information in the records.--The information in the records corresponds to that in the records of service in the Spanish-American War.

Research aid.--The list of officers printed by Heitman and described under "Records of the Spanish-American War" above includes the officers of the Philippine Insurrection.

Documents Relating to Individuals in Correspondence Files

The records.--Documents in correspondence files that relate to individual volunteer officers are dated primarily 1812-1903. They consist chiefly of letters addressed to the War Department relating to such matters as change in grade, correction of record, and application for medal of honor.

Except for Civil War service, such correspondence is occasionally found in the regular correspondence files described above under "Military Service Records of the Regular Army." Documents relating to volunteer service in the Civil War and later are interfiled in the bound series of letters received by the Volunteer Service Division of The Adjutant General's Office, 1861-89. There are 71 volumes of registers of these letters and 28 volumes of alphabetical indexes to them. In addition, there is a related series of letters sent for the same period, together with 65 volumes of alphabetical name indexes. Many documents relating to a soldier are filed together irrespective of date.

Use of the records.--These records are time consuming to use unless the approximate date of a letter is known.

RECORD GROUP

The military records of volunteer organizations are in Record Group 94, Records of The Adjutant General's Office.

MISCELLANEOUS MILITARY RECORDS, 1784-1815

These records consist of Post-Revolutionary War manuscripts; miscellaneous records of the War of 1812; and prisoner-of-war records of the War of 1812.

Post-Revolutionary War Manuscripts

The records.--Dated 1784-1811, these records consist of miscellaneous muster rolls, accounts, and related materials. They are filed in 100 envelopes.

Index to the records.--There is a master name index on cards.

Information in the records.--A document shows such information as the name, rank, and military organization of a soldier and is usually dated.

Miscellaneous Records of the War of 1812

The records.--These records, dated 1812-15, include disbursement papers, pay receipts, and related correspondence. They are filed in numbered jacket-envelopes.

Index to the records.--There is a master name index on cards.

Information in the records.--A document includes such information as the name, rank, and military organization of a soldier and the date when a payment was made or due.

Prisoner-of-war Records of the War of 1812

The records.--These records, dated 1812-15, include miscellaneous correspondence relating to both British and American prisoners in numerically arranged bundles that are separately indexed on cards; correspondence and lists of prisoners sent from the Treasury Department to the Adjutant General's Office, arranged numerically and indexed separately on cards; unarranged and unindexed lists of prisoners sent from the Navy Department to the Adjutant General's Office; and a list of American prisoners of war held at Quebec, Halifax, Nova Scotia, and the West Indies, with entries arranged alphabetically under place of imprisonment, with two alphabetical sequences under Halifax.

Information in the records.--The records vary considerably as to detail but include such information as the name and often the rank and military organization of the prisoner, the date and place of his capture, and the date of his release.

RECORD GROUPS

These miscellaneous military records are in Record Group 94, Records of The Adjutant General's Office.

CIVIL WAR DRAFT RECORDS

The National Archives has the draft records of the Civil War. They were created in accordance with an act approved March 3, 1863 (12 Stat. 731) and relate to men residing in the part of the United States under Union control. They include the consolidated lists of the Washington office, and the descriptive rolls of the enrollment districts.

Consolidated Lists

The records.--The consolidated lists are the principal records of the Washington office of the Provost Marshal General's Bureau relating to individual men. They are arranged by name of State and thereunder by enrollment or Congressional district. Most of them are bound in volumes. They are divided into classes as follows: (1) Persons subject to military duty between the ages of 20 and 35 years and unmarried persons subject to military duty above the age of 35 years and under the age of 45; (2) married men aged above 35 and under 45; and (3) volunteers. Entries in each class are arranged alphabetically by the initial letter of the surname.

Information in the records.--An entry shows for each man his name, place of residence, age as of July 1, 1863, occupation, marital status, the State, territory, or country of his birth, and, if a volunteer, the designation of his military organization.

Descriptive Rolls

The records.--The descriptive rolls or lists are the principal records of the enrollment districts relating to individual men. They are arranged by name of State, thereunder by number of enrollment or Congressional district. The rolls are chiefly in the form of bound volumes. The arrangement of the entries varies considerably from district to district. Some are not indexed; some are indexed by initial letter of surname; and some are indexed according to place of residence.

Information in the records.--An entry often shows, in addition to the information in the corresponding consolidated list, the personal description of the man listed, the exact place of his birth, and evidence as to whether he was accepted or rejected for military service. The entries in many volumes, however, are not completely filled out.

Use of the records.--To use either the consolidated lists or the descriptive rolls, the Congressional district in which a man lived needs to be known. If the county in which he lived in 1863 is known, the number of the Congressional district in which the county was located can be ascertained from Congress, Congressional Directory for the Second Session of the Thirty-Eighth Congress of the United States of America (Washington, 1865). A photocopy of this directory is in the central search room.

RECORD GROUP

The Civil War draft records are in Record Group 110, Records of the Provost Marshal General's Bureau, 1863-66.

BURIAL RECORDS OF SOLDIERS

The National Archives has burial records maintained by the Office of the Quartermaster General, 1862-1939. They were created chiefly in connection with the administration of section 18 of an act of July 17, 1862 (12 Stat. 596), and related acts. They concern soldiers who were buried during the years 1775-1939 but chiefly soldiers who died in service during the Civil War and World War I. They include records of burials at U.S. military installations, chiefly 1861-1914; applications for headstones, dated 1879-1925; card records of World War I soldiers who died overseas, 1917-20; and case files, 1915-39.

Records of Burials at U.S. Military Installations

These records, dated chiefly 1861-1914, include burial registers, and compiled lists of Union soldiers buried at the U.S. Soldiers' Home, and compiled lists of Union soldiers buried at national cemeteries.

Burial Registers

The records.--The registers contain records of burials, 1861-1914, with a few as late as 1939, at the U.S. Soldiers' Home at Washington, the national cemeteries, forts, and post cemeteries in Cuba, the Philippine Islands, Puerto Rico, and China. Filed with the registers are a very few registers for burials at private cemeteries. Most of the registers are arranged alphabetically by name of installation, and they are listed in a checklist.

The most detailed registers are those for the U.S. Soldiers' Home, which are in 4 volumes dated 1861-68. The first 2 volumes, dated 1861-63, contain 7,312 numbered entries, and the second 2 volumes, dated 1864-68, contain 7,371 entries numbered in a second series. Each volume is indexed by initial letter of surname.

Information in the records.--The arrangement, inclusive dates, and contents of the burial registers vary considerably. As a minimum they show for each soldier his name, his military organization, and the date and place of his burial. The registers for the U.S. Soldiers' Home also show the soldier's rank; the town, county, and State of residence before enlistment; the name and residence of his widow, relative, or friend; his age; his nativity; the cause, date, and place of his death; the date of his burial; and, sometimes, the place of his burial.

Compiled Lists of Union Soldiers Buried at the U. S. Soldiers' Home

The records.--These lists relate to burials, 1861-1918. The entries are arranged alphabetically by initial letter of the surname. There is a separate set of lists arranged by name of State.

Information in the records.--An entry usually shows the name of the soldier, his military organization, the date of his death, and the place of his burial.

Compiled List of Union Soldiers Buried at National Cemeteries

The records.--These lists relate chiefly to burials during the years 1861-65 but to some as late as 1886. They are arranged alphabetically by name of State of burial. The lists for each State are divided into three parts, on one of which the names are arranged by name of cemetery, on another by name of military organization, and on another alphabetically by initial letter of surname of soldier. There are lists arranged by surname, however, only for Connecticut, Delaware, District of Columbia, Iowa, Maine, Maryland, Massachusetts, Michigan, New Hampshire, New Jersey, Pennsylvania, Rhode Island, Vermont, and Wisconsin.

Information in the records.--An entry usually shows the name of the soldier, his military organization, the date of his death, and the place of his burial.

Research aid.--Lists of Union soldiers who were buried in public and private cemeteries during the Civil War are published in Quartermaster General's Office, Roll of Honor . . . (Washington, 1865-71). Entries are arranged by name of cemetery, thereunder alphabetically by name of soldier, and show the date of death. Accompanying the volumes is a place index to volumes 1-13 entitled Alphabetical Index to Places of Interment of Deceased Union Soldiers (1868). The National Archives has an unpublished place index to all volumes.

Related information.--The Memorial Division, Quartermaster General's Office, Washington 25, D. C., has an alphabetically arranged 5" x 8" card record identifying practically all soldiers who were buried in national cemeteries and other cemeteries under its jurisdiction from 1861 to the present time.

Applications for Headstones

The records.--The applications for headstones are dated 1879-1925 and relate to servicemen who were buried in private village or city cemeteries. Under terms of an act approved February 3, 1879 (20 Stat. 281), headstones were erected by the Government at the graves of Union servicemen. Headstones were erected later at the graves of servicemen of the Revolutionary War and other wars in which the United States engaged.

Most of the applications are arranged by name of State of burial, thereunder by name of county, thereunder by date of application. A few of the applications that relate to servicemen who were buried at the branches of the National Home for Disabled Volunteer Soldiers are arranged by name of branch, thereunder by date of application.

Indexes.--Alphabetically arranged cards, 3 1/4" x 4", identify the applications dated 1879-1903. Each card shows the name of the serviceman, his military organization, the name and location of the cemetery where he was buried, the date and place of his death, and the date of the application.

Information in the records.--Each application shows the name of the serviceman, his rank and military organization, the date of his death, the name and location of the cemetery in which he was buried, and the name and address of the applicant for the headstone.

Related information.--Later applications for headstones are in the Federal Records Center, Alexandria, Va. They include applications for headstones for Confederate veterans, created in accordance with an act of Congress approved February 26, 1929 (45 Stat. 1307). Many applications or copies of applications are, however, interfiled with the case files described below.

Case Files

The records.--The case files, 1915-39, consist of correspondence and filled-out forms filed in folders, each folder relating to an existing or proposed burial place of a serviceman in the United States. The folders are arranged alphabetically. Although most of the folders relate to servicemen who died between the inclusive dates of the files, some relate to servicemen who died before and some relate to soldiers who were living when the documents were dated. The files include many types of documents relating to burial including copies of applications for headstones.

Each file shows such information as the name of the soldier, his military organization, his place of residence, the date of his death, and the place of his burial.

Card Records of World War I Soldiers Who Died Overseas

These records, on 5" x 8" cards, 1917-20, are arranged alphabetically in two separate series. They consist chiefly of grave registrations but include records of American names in European chapels.

Grave Registrations

Each card shows the name of the soldier, his military organization, the cause and date of his death, the date and place of his burial, and the name and address of his nearest kin or guardian.

Records of American Names in European Chapels

Each card usually shows the name of the soldier, his military organization, the date of his death, a statement that he was killed in action, the name and address of his nearest kin or guardian, and the name of the chapel in which his name appears.

RECORD GROUP

The burial records of soldiers are in Record Group 92, Records of the Office of The Quartermaster General.

RECORDS OF BIRTHS, MARRIAGES, AND CIVILIAN DEATHS AT ARMY POSTS

The records.--The records of births, marriages, and deaths of civilians at army posts are dated 1884-1912. They are abstracts on cards of reports sent by the posts to the Adjutant General's Office. The cards recording each type of information are filed separately and are arranged alphabetically by name of person.

Information in the records.--Each birth card shows the name and sex of the baby; the name, rank, and military organization of the father; the maiden name of the mother; the number of children by the marriage; and the date and place of birth. Each marriage card shows the name and rank or occupation of the husband; the name, age, and place of birth of the wife; and the date and place of marriage. Each death card shows the name of the civilian who died; the name and, where appropriate, the rank and military organization of the husband or nearest relative; the sex and age of the civilian who died; and the date, place, and cause of death.

RECORD GROUP

The records of births, marriages, and civilian deaths are in Record Group 94, Records of The Adjutant General's Office.

GENERAL OBSERVATIONS

An inventory published by the National Archives of the records of The Adjutant General's Office (Washington, 1949; Preliminary Inventory No. 17) identifies most of the military service records of the Regular Army and of volunteer organizations and many related records not described here.

For information about wars and battles up to the end of the 19th century, consult Newton A. Strait, Alphabetical List of Battles, 1754-1900, . . . (Washington, 1900).

For information about Army officer personnel separated between June 30, 1917, and October 6, 1945, and of Army enlisted personnel separated between October 31, 1912, and October 6, 1945, including Army Air Corps and Army Air Force personnel, address the Army Branch, Military Personnel Records Center, GSA, 9700 Page Boulevard, St. Louis 32, Mo. The Air Force Branch of this Center at the same address has information about Air Force officer and enlisted personnel separated since September 1947. For information about Army officer and enlisted personnel separated since October 6, 1945, and Army Air Force personnel separated between October 6, 1945, and September 1947, address the Army Records Center, Department of the Army, 9700 Page Boulevard, St. Louis 32, Mo.

IV. UNITED STATES NAVAL AND MARINE RECORDS

The National Archives has many records relating to officers and men of the United States Navy and Marine Corps. They are dated 1776-1942, but chiefly 1798-1885. They include service records of the Revolutionary War, 1776-83; service records of the Navy, 1798-1885, with some as early as 1794 and as late as 1930; and service records of the Marine Corps, chiefly 1798-1895, with some as late as 1941.

SERVICE RECORDS OF THE REVOLUTIONARY WAR

The service records of the Revolutionary War are very fragmentary. They include record books assembled by the Navy Department, unbound papers assembled by the Navy Department, and records assembled by the War Department.

Record Books Assembled by the Navy Department

The records.--The record books assembled by the Navy Department include the payroll of the Continental Ship *Confederacy*, 1780-81, in one volume; photostat copies of the rosters of the officers and crews of the *Bonhomme Richard*, the *Pallas*, and the *Vengeance*, 1779, in one volume; and photostat copies of the log of the Continental Ship *Ranger*, 1778-80, in one volume.

Indexes.--There is a separate typed index to each volume.

Information in the records.--The information varies from volume to volume. The volumes do contain, however, the names of individuals and the names of the vessels on which they served and sometimes other service or payment data.

Unbound Papers Assembled by the Navy Department

The records.--The unbound papers assembled by the Navy Department that relate to Revolutionary War service form part of a large "area file" of loose papers. The papers vary widely in form and content.

Indexes to the records.--Documents that contain references to naval men of the Revolutionary War, along with other early parts of the area file, are covered by an index on 5" x 3" cards.

Information in the records.--The records show such information as the name and rank of a naval man, the name of the vessel on which he served, and a date.

Records Assembled or Compiled by the War Department

The records.--Among records assembled by the Adjutant General's

Office relating to the Revolutionary War, described in the preceding chapter, are a few pertaining to naval personnel. They consist chiefly of volume 175, which concerns payments for Revolutionary War service to commissioned officers, midshipmen, seamen, and others. The information in these records has been abstracted on cards so that one card contains all the information about one man that is in the original entry. The cards have been placed in jacket-envelopes, which have been alphabetized in a subseries headed "Naval" among the compiled military service records.

Indexes to the records.--The names on the cards have been indexed on the master name index to the compiled military service records, which has been microfilmed.

Information in the records.--The records show such information as the name of the man, his rank or rating, the inclusive dates of his service, and the amount due for naval service.

Research aids.--For identification of some Revolutionary War officers, see Edward W. Callahan, ed., List of Officers of the Navy of the United States and of the Marine Corps, from 1775 to 1900, p. 8, 9 (New York, 1901). Many naval men served in the Revolutionary War from Massachusetts and Virginia. For information about these men see Massachusetts, Secretary of the Commonwealth, Massachusetts Soldiers and Sailors of the Revolutionary War (Boston, 1896-1908); and Gaius M. Brumbaugh, Revolutionary War Records . . . Virginia (Washington, 1936).

For information about French participants see Les Combattants français de la Guerre Américaine, 1778-1783, republished in the United States as Senate Document 77 of the 58th Congress, 2d session (serial 4595).

RECORD GROUPS

The service records of the Revolutionary War are in Record Group 45, Naval Records Collection of the Office of Naval Records and Library, except the records assembled or compiled by the War Department, which are in Record Group 93, War Department Collection of Revolutionary War Records.

Related information.--The Marine Corps, Washington 25, D. C., has compiled information about some marines who served during the Revolutionary War.

SERVICE RECORDS OF THE NAVY

The service records of the United States Navy are dated chiefly 1798-1885, but a few concern the embryonic Navy that began in 1794 and some are dated as late as 1930. They relate to commissioned officers, midshipmen or cadets, enlisted men, and naval apprentices.

Records Relating to Commissioned Officers

These records concern officers of the Regular Navy and acting or volunteer officers who served during the Civil War and Spanish-American War. They include the following series: statements of the place of birth of officers, 1816; statements of the place of birth and residence of officers, 1826; record of officers serving in 1829; statements of service written by officers, 1842-43; age certificates of officers, 1862-63; records of officers in lettered volumes, 1798-1893; records of officers in numbered volumes, 1861-1924; register of engineer officers, 1843-99; biographies of officers, 1865; and personnel record cards of officers of the Naval Auxiliary Service, chiefly 1908-17.

Statements of the Place of Birth of Officers, 1816

The records.--These statements were prepared in response to a Navy Department order of August 1, 1816. They are in one volume and relate almost entirely to officers whose surnames began with C and D.

Information in the records.--Each statement includes such information as the name, age or date of birth of the officer, and the place of birth.

Statements of the Place of Birth and Residence of Officers, 1826

The records.--These statements are filled-out forms, most of which are arranged alphabetically in two volumes. Those relating to chaplains and pursers are bound in a separate volume with other records.

Information in the records.--Each statement shows the name of the officer and the name of the State or territory in which he was born, from which he was appointed, and of which he was a citizen.

Record of Officers Serving in 1829

The records.--The record of officers serving in 1829 is in one indexed volume.

Information in the records.--Each entry shows the name of the officer and his service record from the date of his appointment to 1829.

Statements of Service Written by Officers, 1842-43

The records.--The statements of service were written on forms by the officers largely from memory and in response to questionnaires. They are in two indexed volumes. Two separate volumes contain letters of transmittal and supplemental biographical statements of some officers.

Information in the records.--Each form shows the name and service record of each officer then in service from the beginning of his service to December 31, 1842.

Age Certificates of Officers

The records.--The age certificates of officers, both Naval and Marine, were prepared as a result of the retirement provisions of an act of Congress approved December 21, 1861 (12 Stat. 329). The certificates are in four volumes, two for 1862, and two for 1863. The entries in each series are arranged alphabetically by surname of officer and are indexed.

Information in the records.--Each certificate is signed by the officer and shows his name, rank, and date of birth.

Records of Officers in Lettered Volumes

The records.--The records of officers in lettered volumes relate to most officers (including volunteer officers of the Civil War and noncommissioned officers) who served at any time during the period 1798-1893. They are abstracts of service records and refer to the series of letters sent conveying appointments and orders and accepting resignations and the applications for appointment as midshipman or cadet.

A list of the lettered volumes with the inclusive dates of the years covered by each follows:

A 1798-1801	F 1818-25	K 1859-63
B 1801-3	G 1825-31	L 1864-71
C 1804-8	H 1832-40	M 1872-78
D 1809-13	I 1840-45	N 1879-88
E 1813-17	J 1846-58	O 1889-93

There are two parts to volumes J through O, each part being separately bound. Part I relates to officers above the rank of master, and part 2 to officers of the rank of master or below. Some volumes are indexed; in others the entries are arranged alphabetically.

Information in the records.--An entry shows the name of the officer, the date of his appointment, the date and nature of changes in rank, and, where pertinent, the date and nature of the termination of his service.

Records of Officers in Numbered Volumes

The records.--The records of officers in numbered volumes relate to many officers of the Regular Navy, but chiefly those who were appointed between 1846 and 1902. The 38 volumes contain entries as late as 1924.

Index.--There is a loose-leaf index to the names in these volumes.

Information in the records.--The records often show such information as the name of the officer, the date and place of his birth, the date of his entrance on duty, the ranks he held, the names of the stations to which he was assigned, his place of residence, the date and place of his death, and, if he was serving in 1908 or later, the names and addresses of beneficiaries.

Register of Engineer Officers

The records.--The register of engineer officers is one indexed volume, 1843-99. It relates to the officers who served in the Engineer Corps of the Navy until the Corps was abolished by an act approved March 3, 1899 (30 Stat. 1004).

Information in the records.--Each entry shows the name of the officer, the date and place of his birth, the date of his appointment to the Engineer Corps, a detailed service record, and the date and place of his death or the date of his retirement.

Biographies of Officers

The records.--The biographies of officers relate chiefly to the Civil War and are in three indexed volumes, prepared about 1865, and are very incomplete. They vary considerably in their detail and some appear to be autobiographical. They cite wounds received.

Personnel Record Cards of Officers of the Naval Auxiliary Service

The records.--The personnel record cards of officers of the Naval Auxiliary Service, chiefly 1907-17, are arranged alphabetically by name of officer.

Information in the records.--Each card shows the name of the officer, his place of residence, the place and date of his birth, the name and address of his next of kin, and a summary of his service record.

Research aids.--For an alphabetical list of the names of the officers of the Regular Navy and of the acting or volunteer officers of the Civil War with an identification of each, see Edward W. Callahan, ed., List of Officers of the Navy of the United States and of the Marine Corps, from 1775 to 1900, p. 15-609 (New York, 1901). For information about officers who served since 1900, see Navy Department, Register of the Commissioned and Warrant Officers of the United States Navy and Marine Corps, an annual publication variously titled.

For information about each officer who served in the Barbary Wars, see Office of Naval Records and Library, Register of Officer Personnel, United States Navy and Marine Corps and Ships' Data, 1801-1807 (Washington, 1945). This volume, which gives the name and brief service record for each commissioned, warrant, and acting officer in the Navy and Marine Corps during those years, supplements the Naval Documents Related to the United States Wars With the Barbary Powers (Washington, 1939-44).

For information about many naval men who served in the Civil War, see Navy Department, Official Records of the Union and Confederate Navies in the War of the Rebellion, General Index (Washington, 1927; also published as H. Doc. 113, 69th Cong., 1st sess., serial 8603). This consists in part of a personal name index to 30 volumes of transcripts of official records.

For further information about the records described above, and related records, see National Archives, Preliminary Checklist of the Naval Records Collection of the Office of Naval Records and Library, 1775-1910 (Washington, 1945) and Preliminary Inventory of the Records of the Bureau of Naval Personnel (Washington, 1960). Note particularly item 466 in the former, which is an index to records relating in part to a few War of 1812 officers. Applications for appointment and testimonial letters for advancement are in numerous subseries in Record Group 24, described in the inventory.

Related information.--For information about officers who served after 1885, address the Bureau of Naval Personnel, Department of the Navy, Washington 25, D. C.

RECORD GROUPS

The statements of place of birth of officers and of place of birth and residence, the register of engineer officers, and the biographies of officers are in Record Group 45, Naval Records Collection of the Office of Naval Records and Library. The record of officers serving in 1829, the age certificates of officers, the records of officers in lettered volumes and in numbered volumes, and the personnel record cards of officers of the Naval Auxiliary Service are in Record Group 24, Records of the Bureau of

Naval Personnel. Part of the statements of service written by officers are in Record Group 45 and part are in Record Group 24.

Records Relating to Midshipmen or Cadets

The records relating to midshipmen or cadets concern chiefly those who served from the time of the establishment of the United States Naval Academy at Annapolis. They include registers of admissions and records of appointees.

Registers of Admissions

The records.--The registers of admissions, 1849-1930, form a single series of bound volumes. The entries are arranged chronologically according to date of appointment.

Information in the records.--Each entry normally shows the name of the candidate; the date and place of his birth; his signature; and the name, place of residence, and occupation or profession of his parent or guardian. The age instead of the date and place of birth is given in the earliest registers.

Research aid.--See Edward W. Callahan, ed., List of Officers of the Navy of the United States and of the Marine Corps, from 1775 to 1900, p. 15-609 (New York, 1901), or the name index in the Naval Academy, Annapolis, Alumni Association, Register of Graduates, an annual publication. It gives for each graduate his name, the date of his graduation, the name of the State where he was born, his highest rank at time of publication, and, where appropriate, the date of his retirement of death.

Records of Appointees

The records.--The records of appointees, 1862-1910, are in individual jackets arranged numerically and are usually known as jackets of naval cadets. Each jacket includes such documents as a letter of nomination from a Member of Congress, a letter of acceptance, testimonial letters, reports of examining boards, an oath, and a letter of promotion to ensign. Interfiled with the jackets of those who became cadets at the Naval Academy are those of unsuccessful applicants.

Index to the records.--The Bureau of Naval Personnel, Washington 25, D.C., retains the index, but the file numbers of the jackets of midshipmen or cadets for the period 1862-93 can be obtained from the records of officers in the lettered volumes, described above.

Information in the records.--A jacket usually shows such information as the man's name, his place of residence, the name of his father, and, where appropriate, the date of his appointment and the date of his commission as ensign.

RECORD GROUPS

The registers of admissions are in Record Group 181, Records of Naval Districts and Shore Establishments; the records of appointees are in Record Group 24, Records of the Bureau of Naval Personnel.

Related information.--Information about the relatively few midshipmen in the U.S. Navy during the years 1798-1848 is meager. Some information may be obtained from the records of officers in lettered volumes, described above, and from the general correspondence files.

Records Relating to Enlisted Men

The records relating to enlisted men are dated chiefly 1798-1885 with some as late as 1919. They include muster rolls and pay rolls of vessels, 1798-1844, and later; muster rolls and pay rolls of shore establishments, chiefly 1800-1842; registers of enlistments, chiefly 1845-1854; weekly returns of enlistments at naval rendezvous, 1855-91; quarterly returns of enlistments on vessels, 1866-91; jackets for enlisted men who served during the years 1842-85; personnel record cards for enlisted men of the Naval Auxiliary Service, chiefly 1913-17; and card abstracts of World War I service records, 1917-19.

Muster Rolls and Pay Rolls of Vessels

The records.--The muster rolls and pay rolls of vessels for the years 1798-1844 and later are in bound volumes. Each volume normally relates to a single vessel for a specific period of service. The volumes are arranged alphabetically by name of vessel, and the entries in each volume are arranged chronologically.

Indexes to the records.--For each of the first three volumes of the muster rolls and pay rolls of the Frigate Constitution, 1798-1815, there is a typed name index.

Information in the records.--An entry shows normally the name of the enlisted man, the name of the vessel on which he was serving, and the date of service. Some entries show the name of the vessel from which the man came and the name of the vessel to which he was assigned.

Use of the records.--If an enlisted man served on the Frigate Constitution, it sometimes is possible from the reference to his name to trace his naval career. Lists of vessels for which there are muster rolls and pay rolls are published in National Archives, Preliminary Checklist of the Naval Records Collection of the Office of Naval Records and Library, 1775-1910, p. 111-114 (Washington, 1945). A list of naval vessels, 1797-1900, also appears in Edward W. Callahan, ed., List of Officers of the Navy of the United States and of the Marine Corps, from 1775 to 1900, p. 725-750 (New York, 1901).

Muster Rolls and Pay Rolls of Shore Establishments

The records.--The muster rolls and pay rolls of shore establishments, dated chiefly 1800-1842, are in bound volumes. Each volume relates to one or more shore establishments. The volumes are arranged alphabetically by name of shore establishment, and the entries in each volume are arranged chronologically.

Information in the records.--Each entry shows such information as the name of the enlisted man, the date of his appearance at the shore establishment, the name of the vessel or shore establishment from which he came, his rating, the date of his leaving the vessel or shore establishment, and the reason.

747-596 O - 64 - 6

Registers of Enlistments

The records.--The registers of enlistments are the chief source of data about enlisted men for the years 1845-54. For this period they are in three bound volumes (two volumes for 1845-53 and one volume for 1854) with entries that have been copied in part from records later destroyed. The entries are arranged alphabetically by initial letter of the surname.

Indexes to the records.--The records were indexed and the index was incorporated in a master index to records of enlisted men on microfilm. One part of this index, amounting to 32 rolls, relates to enlistment records for the years 1845-84 except for the Civil War. The original index is no longer extant.

Information in the records.--Each entry shows the name of the enlisted man, the date and place of his enlistment, the place of his birth, and his age. For some entries a column for remarks is filled out with such information as the name of the ship or station assigned or the date of discharge.

Weekly Returns of Enlistments at Naval Rendezvous

The records.--The weekly returns of enlistments at naval rendezvous, 1855-91, are the chief source of data for enlisted men for the years 1855-65 and are important sources for the years 1866-85. Entries are in bound volumes, which are arranged by year, thereunder by week, thereunder by name of naval rendezvous, thereunder by date of enlistment. The returns for each year are numbered consecutively.

Indexes to the records.--The records for the period 1855-84 were indexed and the index was incorporated into the master index on microfilm, mentioned above. A series of 32 rolls of microfilm relates to service during the years 1845-84 except in the Civil War. Another series of 31 rolls relates to Civil War service. For 1885 there is a key to enlistment returns which contains entries arranged alphabetically to the first letter of the surname.

Information in the records.--Each entry in the weekly returns of enlistments normally shows under the name of the naval rendezvous the name of the enlisted man, the date and term of his enlistment, his rating, a reference to his previous naval service if any, the place of his birth, his age, his occupation, and his personal description. Some entries show place of residence.

Quarterly Returns of Enlistments on Vessels

The records.--The quarterly returns of enlistments on vessels, 1866-91, are also an important source for data about enlisted men, 1866-84. Entries are in bound volumes, which are arranged by year, thereunder by quarter, thereunder by name of vessel, thereunder by date of enlistment.

Indexes to the records.--The records for the years 1866-84 were indexed and the index was incorporated in the master index described under weekly returns of enlistments at naval rendezvous.

Information in the records.--Each entry normally shows under the name of the vessel the name of the enlisted man, the date and term of his enlistment, his rating, a reference to his previous naval service if any, the place of his birth, his age, his occupation, and his personal description. Some entries show place of residence.

Jackets for Enlisted Men

The records.--These records relate to service performed between 1842 and 1885 by many enlisted men. The jackets, which are arranged alphabetically, were prepared between 1885 and 1941 to contain documents assembled or created in connection with such matters as pension claims, requests for service records, and requests for copies of honorable discharge.

Information in the records.--A jacket normally shows the name of the enlisted man, his full service record, and the place of his residence after service.

Personnel Record Cards for Enlisted Men of the Naval Auxiliary Service

The records.--The personnel record cards for enlisted men of the Naval Auxiliary Service are dated chiefly 1913-17. They are arranged alphabetically by name.

Information in the records.--A card shows the name of the enlisted man, his rating, the name of the vessel on which he served, the year and place of his birth, his occupation, his personal description, the name of his next of kin, the date and nature of his separation from the service, and the place of his residence.

Card Abstracts of World War I Service Records

The records.--These card abstracts are 5" x 8" in size and are dated 1917-19. They are arranged alphabetically by name of State and thereunder alphabetically by name of enlisted man.

Information in the records.--A card shows the name of the enlisted man, his serial number, the date and place of his enrollment or enlistment, his age and rating, his home address, the dates and places of his service, and the date and place of his discharge.

RECORD GROUPS

The records are in Record Group 24, Records of the Bureau of Naval Personnel, except muster rolls and pay rolls of vessels and shore establishments, which are in Record Group 45, Naval Records Collection of the Office of Naval Records and Library.

Related information.--For information about enlisted men who served after 1885, address the Navy Branch, Military Personnel Record Center, GSA, 9700 Page Boulevard, St. Louis 32, Mo.

Records Relating to Naval Apprentices

The records relating to naval apprentices are dated chiefly 1837-89. They are based on an act approved March 2, 1837 (5 Stat. 153) that provided that boys between the ages of 13 and 18 could enlist and serve until they were 21. The provisions of the act were revived in 1864 after periods of nonuse. The records include certificates of consent, 1838-40; apprenticeship papers, 1864-89; and a register of naval apprentices, 1864-75.

Certificates of Consent

The records.--These records consist of one volume, not indexed, dated 1838-40.

Information in the records.--A certificate shows the name of the boy, the date of his birth, and the name of his parent or guardian.

Apprenticeship Papers

The records.--The apprenticeship papers, 1864-89, are in individual folders arranged alphabetically by the first two letters of the surname. They consist of forms filled out by parents or guardians and, for the years 1864-69, include testimonials as to character.

Information in the records.--Each apprenticeship paper shows the name of the apprentice, the place of his service, the date of his entrance into the service, the name and residence of his parent or guardian, the place and date of birth of the apprentice, and the relationship between the apprentice and the parent or guardian.

Register of Naval Apprentices

The records.--The register of naval apprentices, 1864-75, is a single volume indexed by initial letter of the surname. It concerns service aboard the training ships Sabine, Portsmouth, and Saratoga.

Information in the records.--An entry shows the name of the apprentice, the date and place of his birth, the date and place of enlistment, the name of his parent or guardian, and the date of detachment from the service.

RECORD GROUP

The records relating to naval apprentices are in Record Group 24, Records of the Bureau of Naval Personnel.

SERVICE RECORDS OF THE MARINE CORPS

The records.--The National Archives has the service records of the Marine Corps, chiefly for the years 1798-1895, with some as late as 1941. They relate to officers and enlisted men.

Records Relating to Officers

The records relating to officers are scattered among many series including letters of acceptance, 1808-62; age certificates of officers, 1862-63; register of living and retired officers, 1899-1905; and card records of the names of officers who served during the years 1798-1941.

Letters of Acceptance

The records.--The letters of acceptance are dated 1808-62. They are in three partially overlapping volumes. The volume for 1808-16 contains acceptances arranged alphabetically by surname. The two volumes for

1812-62 contain acceptances arranged chronologically. Oaths of allegiance are filed with many of the letters.

Information in the records.--A letter shows the name of the officer, the date of his acceptance of a commission, and, after 1830, the name of the State or Territory in which he was born and from which he was appointed. Some letters show the officer's place of residence.

Age Certificates of Officers

The records.--The age certificates of marine officers are included in the volumes of age certificates of naval officers, 1862-63, described above under "Records relating to Commissioned Officers".

Information in the records.--Each certificate is signed by the officer and shows his name, rank, and date of birth.

Register of Living and Retired Officers

The records.--The register of living and retired officers, 1899-1905, relates chiefly to marine officers who served in the Spanish-American War. It lists each officer serving in 1899 and each officer commissioned during the years 1899-1904. It is an indexed volume.

Information in the records.--An entry shows the name of the officer; the date and place of his birth; the name of the State from which he was appointed; the name of the State in which he was born; and his service record from 1899 to 1905.

Card Records of the Names of Officers

The records.--There are cards (2 1/2" x 3") for officers who served at some time during the period 1798-1941, with a few cards for marines of the Revolutionary War. They are alphabetized by the first few letters of the surname, thereunder by the first few letters of the given name.

Information in the records.--Each card usually shows the name of an officer, the year of appointment and rank or, if year of appointment was 1905 or later, his serial number.

Research aid.--The names of Marine Corps officers with their dates of appointment are given alphabetically in Edward W. Callahan, ed., List of Officers of the Navy of the United States and of the Marine Corps from 1775 to 1900, p. 679-701 (New York, 1901).

Records Relating to Enlisted Men

The records relating to enlisted men include service records, 1798-1895; card abstracts of service records, 1917-18; and card records of the names of enlisted men, chiefly 1798-1941.

Service Records

The records.--The service records, 1798-1895, are in individual jackets, which are arranged by year of enlistment, thereunder by first letter of surname, and thereunder by date of enlistment. A jacket with entries dated before 1821 is usually limited to a typed transcript of information taken from the size rolls. A jacket relating to service after 1820 normally includes an enlistment paper, and often such documents as correspondence, an abstract of the size roll, and a medical record.

Index to the records.--The card records of the names of enlisted men described below serve as an index to the service records.

Information in the records.--The documents in a jacket usually show the name of the enlisted man; the date, place, and term of his enlistment; his age; his personal description; and his occupation. The documents in some jackets show the date and circumstances under which men left the service.

Card Abstracts of Service Records, World War I

The records.--These card abstracts concern the enlisted men of World War I. The cards are 4" x 6" in size and are carbons. They are arranged alphabetically by name of State, thereunder alphabetically by name of enlisted man.

Information in the records.--Each card shows the name of an enlisted man, the place of his residence, the place and date of his enlistment, the place and date of his birth, his rank and advancement in rank, and the date of his separation from the service.

Card Records of the Names of Enlisted Men

The records.--There are cards (2 1/2" x 3") for enlisted men who served at some time during the period 1798-1941, with a few cards for marines of the Revolutionary War. They are alphabetized by the first few letters of the surname, thereunder by the first few letters of the given name.

Information in the records.--Each card usually shows the name of the enlisted man, the date and place of his enlistment, and, if service was in 1905 or later, his serial number.

Use of the records.--Because of the arrangement of the cards, they cannot, as a rule, be used effectively to ascertain the names of all persons of a given surname.

RECORD GROUPS

The records relating to the Marine Corps are in Record Group 127, Records of the United States Marine Corps, except for the letters of acceptance, which are in Record Group 80, General Records of the Department of the Navy, and the age certificates of officers, which are in Record Group 24, Records of the Bureau of Naval Personnel.

Related information.--For detailed study see National Archives, Preliminary Checklist of the Records of the United States Marine Corps, 1798-1944 (Washington, 1946), and Preliminary Checklist of the General Records of the Department of the Navy, 1804-1944 (Washington, 1945), especially item 1. For information from the service records since 1895 for both marine officers and enlisted men, address the Navy Branch, Military Personnel Records Center, GSA, 9700 Page Boulevard, St. Louis 32, Mo.

For officers and enlisted men of the United States Navy and Marine Corps who received the medal of honor, see Bureau of Naval Personnel, Medal of Honor, 1861-1949 (Washington, 1950).

V. RECORDS OF VETERANS' BENEFITS

The National Archives has many noncurrent records of benefits to veterans, their widows, and other heirs. They relate to military, naval, and marine service performed between 1775 and 1934, exclusive of Confederate and World War I service. The benefits included pensions, rights to land, special naval awards, and domiciliary care. The records consist of pension application records, pension payment records,[1] bounty-land warrant application records,[2] claims files for special naval awards, and records of Federal homes. Each kind of record is described below.

PENSION APPLICATION RECORDS

Pensions were granted by Congress to invalid or disabled veterans; to widows and orphans of men who were killed or died in service; to veterans who served a minimum period of time if they were living at an advanced age; to widows of veterans who served a minimum period of time if the widows were living at an advanced age; and, in some instances, to other heirs. Pensions granted on the basis of death or disability incurred in service are known as death or disability pensions. Pensions granted on the basis of service for a minimum period of time are called service pensions.

The acts of Congress under which applications for pensions were made are numerous. They include public acts which affected large groups of persons and private acts which affected specific individuals.

Each claim for a pension was normally based upon a single act of Congress. A claims file consists of the application of the claimant, supporting documents of identity and service, and evidence of the action taken on the claim. There were often two or more claims relating to the service of the same veteran in the same war. For example, a veteran might apply for a pension and, after his death, his widow might apply for a pension on the basis of the same service. A file showing that a surviving widow applied for a pension has normally more information than a veteran's file and is identified by the use of the letter "W" as the first part of the file number.

Initially the documents relating to an individual claim were folded and placed in an annotated jacket. Later these documents were flattened and filed with the jacket in one or more large envelopes. The jacket, now obsolete as a container, was kept because of the annotations on it. The envelopes with their contents are called pension application files. Con-

[1]The pension payment records include the Revolutionary War final payment vouchers that are in part consolidated with the Revolutionary War service series of pension application records described under "Pension Application Records."

[2]Most of the Revolutionary War bounty-land warrant application records and some War of 1812 bounty-land warrant application records are consolidated or interfiled with the related pension application records.

solidated with the documents relating to an original claim and in the same envelope or envelopes are the documents, if any, relating to later pension claims based on the same service. In addition, some bounty-land warrant application files and some final payment vouchers have been consolidated with the related pension application files. The number and nature of documents in a file vary considerably.

The pension application files in the National Archives number many millions. They are divided into the following major series: (1) Revolutionary War invalid series; (2) Revolutionary War service series; (3) "Old Wars" series; (4) War of 1812 series; (5) Mexican War series; (6) Civil War and Later series; and (7) Indian wars series. These records are described separately below.

The records in all the above-mentioned series except those for the Mexican War, the Civil War and later, and the Indian wars are arranged alphabetically by name of veteran. The excepted series are arranged numerically by application or certificate number. All series of pension application files have alphabetical name indexes. There is also a 3" x 5" card index known as the Remarried Widows Index, which is useful in identifying files in all series except those relating to service in the Revolutionary War.

The Remarried Widows Index is in two parts: One covers records relating to claims based on service in the War of 1812, the Mexican War, the Indian wars, and the Regular Establishment before 1861; the other covers records relating to claims based on service in the Civil War and later wars, World War I excepted, and in the Regular Establishment after the Civil War.

Both parts of the Remarried Widows Index are arranged alphabetically by the name of the remarried widow. In addition to the name of the remarried widow, each card gives the name of the veteran who was her former husband, the designation of the military or naval unit with which he served, and the file or certificate number.

Revolutionary War Invalid Series

All Revolutionary War pensions granted before the establishment of the Federal Government were handled by the various States, often pursuant to resolutions of the Continental Congress. By a resolution of June 7, 1785 (Journals of the Continental Congress, 1774-1789, vol. 38, p. 435-37), the Congress of the Confederation asked the States to prepare annual lists of invalid pensioners.[3] Under an act of September 29, 1789 (1 Stat. 95), the Federal Government assumed temporarily--and later permanently--the responsibility for paying these invalid pensions. Under an act of March 23, 1792 (1 Stat. 243), as amended, other veterans were permitted to apply to the Federal Government for invalid pensions. This act permitted disabled veterans to apply for pensions before the United States circuit or district courts in the several States. These applications were transmitted to the War Department, but they were evidently destroyed in the War Department fire of November 8, 1800. Reports based upon these applications were made

[3]The names of persons appearing on these lists are included in the lists of invalid pensioners printed in War Department, Report From the Secretary of War . . . in Relation to the Pension Establishment of the United States, 1835 (23d Cong., 1st sess., S. Doc. 514; serials 249-251), unindexed.

by the War Department for the Congress. There are two partially duplicating sets: reports submitted to Congress; and reports retained by the War Department.

Reports Submitted to Congress

The records.--Eight reports were submitted to Congress during the years 1792-95. A report dated 1792 is in a House of Representatives volume entitled "Reports War Department 1st Cong. 3rd Sess., to 2nd Cong. 2nd Sess." (vol. 2). The seven reports for 1794 and 1795 are in a Senate volume entitled "War Office Returns of Claims to Invalid Pensions." Each report identifies many applicants for invalid pensions. Entries are arranged by date of report, thereunder by name of State, and thereunder by name of applicant.

Information in the records.--Each entry in the 1792 report contains the name of the invalid pensioner, his rank, his regiment, the nature of his disability, and the date of the commencement of the pension. Each entry in the 1794 and 1795 reports contains the name of the invalid applicant; his rank; his regiment, company, or ship; the date and place of his becoming disabled; the place of his residence at the date of the report; and, as a rule, evidence of action on the claim.

Research aid.--All eight reports have been transcribed, printed, and indexed in U. S. Congress, American State Papers, Class 9, Claims, p. 58-67, 85-122, 125-128, 135-145, and 150-172 (Washington, Gales and Seaton, 1834). Each entry in the volume has been transcribed on an individual sheet of paper, and the sheets have been placed in separate envelopes, which are interfiled with the Revolutionary War service series described below.

Reports Retained by the War Department

The records.-- The reports retained by the War Department are dated 1794-96. They constitute pages 527-612 of a War Department record book, the backstrip inscription of which reads "War Office Letter Book 1791-94." The entries in the reports duplicate many entries in the reports submitted to Congress.

Information in the records.--Most of the entries in the War Department reports, 1794-96, contain essentially the same types of information that are found in the reports of 1794 and 1795 submitted to Congress.

Research aid.--The 1796 reports have been transcribed and printed in the National Genealogical Society Quarterly, vol. 46, nos. 1 and 2 (March and June 1958). The continuing article in these two issues of the Quarterly is entitled "Recently Discovered Records Relating to Revolutionary War Veterans Who Applied for Pensions under the Act of 1792."

Revolutionary War Service Series

The records.--The Revolutionary War service series consists of pension application records created chiefly under acts of Congress dating between 1818 and 1853. The earliest act, approved March 18, 1818 (3 Stat. 410), applied to veterans of the continental establishment and the naval service who had served a minimum of 9 months. Its effectiveness was greatly curtailed by an act of Congress approved May 1, 1820 (3 Stat. 569), which provided that the pensioners submit property schedules proving that they were needy. The most liberal act was an act approved June 7, 1832

(4 Stat. 529), which provided that veterans with 6 months' service, irrespective of the type of service and irrespective of need, were entitled to apply for pensions. Beginning with an act approved July 4, 1836 (5 Stat. 127), widows of veterans with the requisite minimum service were entitled to pensions provided that they had married the veterans before the expiration of the last period of the veterans' service. Other acts provided pensions for widows who married veterans at later dates; finally an act approved February 3, 1853 (10 Stat. 154), allowed pensions to widows irrespective of the dates of marriage. Because of the absence of many of the official records of the Revolutionary War, it was often necessary for an applicant to submit evidence of service and identity such as a certificate of discharge or a commission, an affidavit of a comrade in arms, or a leaf from a family Bible with family data.

The files are arranged alphabetically by name of veteran. Interfiled with or consolidated within the individual files of the Revolutionary War service series are the following related materials: transcripts of the invalid pension reports described above under "Revolutionary War Invalid Series"; most of the Revolutionary War bounty-land warrant application records and the large record cards relating to bounty-land warrant application records that were destroyed by fire, described below under "Bounty-Land Warrant Application Records"; and some final payment vouchers described below under "Pension Payment Records, Treasury Department Records of Payments to Revolutionary War and Other Pensioners."

The records contain appropriate cross references to the half-pay files of Virginia naval officers described later in this chapter under "Claims Files for Special Naval Awards." Select documents in some files, such as commissions, discharge papers, diaries, and family Bibles submitted with the claims as evidence, have been segregated for historical purposes, but appropriate cross references have been made in the files. Some documents were segregated and transferred to the Library of Congress in 1909 pursuant to an act of Congress approved February 25, 1903 (32 Stat. 865).

Indexes to the records.--An alphabetical name index to the Revolutionary War pension application files has appeared serially beginning March 1943 in the *National Genealogical Society Quarterly*. The index does not, however, include entries relating to transcripts of the 1796 reports on invalid pensioners described above under the Revolutionary War invalid series in the section on "Reports Retained by the War Department." The printed index covering entries for the files of veterans whose surnames begin with the letters A through S is available on microfilm. Also reproduced on microfilm are the face sides of jackets (envelopes) or record cards relating to veterans whose surnames begin with the letters T through Z.

The printed and microfilmed indexes show the name of the veteran; the State from which he served, provided the service was other than that rendered with the Continental Line or naval forces; the name of his widow in appropriate instances; and the pension application file number and/or the bounty-land warrant application file number. (The Revolutionary War bounty-land warrant application files are described later.)

Information in the records.--A pension application file shows the name, rank, military or naval unit, and period of service of the veteran. If he applied for a pension, it shows his age or date of birth, place of birth, and place of residence. If the widow applied, it shows the date and place of his death, her age and the place of her residence, the date and place of her marriage to the veteran, and her maiden name.

Research aids.--There are several published lists of value in identifying Revolutionary War pensioners. The Revolutionary War and other pensioners who were or had been on the rolls are listed by name of State or Territory in War Department, Report From the Secretary of War, . . . in Relation to the Pension Establishment of the United States, 1835 (23d Cong., 1st sess., S. Doc. 514; serials 249-251), unindexed. Volume 1 lists the names of pensioners residing in New England; volume 2, those residing in New York, New Jersey, Pennsylvania, Delaware, Maryland, and Virginia; and volume 3, all others.

The names of pensioners on the rolls in 1840 were obtained from the population census schedules. The pensioners are listed by name with age in Department of State, A Census of Pensioners for Revolutionary or Military Services (Washington, 1841), an unindexed volume, which was reprinted in 1954. Entries are arranged by name of State or Territory, thereunder by name of county, and, in the case of some counties, by name of minor subdivision. Some entries, however, do not relate to Federal pensioners and may refer to State pensioners.

The Genealogical Society of the Church of Jesus Christ of Latter-Day Saints has prepared a typescript index to the names appearing in the publication just cited. The Society also has a negative microfilm copy of the index. The National Archives Library also has a typescript copy and a microfilm copy of the index.

For an alphabetical list of some abstracts of pension application files and citations to publications in which the abstracts have been published, consult Donald Lines Jacobus, Index to Genealogical Periodicals, vol. 2, p. 102-115 (New Haven, 1948).

"Old War" Series

The records.--The "Old Wars" (or "Old War") series of pension application files relates to claims based on death or disability incurred in service rendered between the end of the Revolutionary War (April 11, 1783) and April 14, 1862, but not including service in the War of 1812. The claims concern service in the Mexican War, Indian wars, and, in the case of some military and naval servicemen, the Civil War. They also concern service in the Regular Establishment. Numerous acts of Congress were passed under which these applications were made, the first one being an act approved April 30, 1790 (1 Stat. 119).

The "Old Wars" series of pension application records consists of several subseries: Mexican War death or disability files; Civil War death or disability files; and miscellaneous death or disability files, which relate to claims based on service in the Indian wars and in the Regular Establishment.

Some "Old Wars" pension application files have been consolidated with the pension application files in the separate series of pension application records for the Mexican War and the Indian wars, described later.

Within each of the "Old Wars" subseries the files are arranged alphabetically by name of veteran.

Indexes to the records.--An alphabetical name index is reproduced on microfilm. The index shows the name of the veteran; the name and class of dependent, if any; service data; and the application or file number and, for an approved claim, a certificate number and the State from which the claim was made. Certain files in the "Old War" series can be located through the use of the Remarried Widows Index, described earlier.

Information in the records.--A file shows the name, rank, military or naval unit, and period of service of the veteran. If he applied for a pension, it shows his age or date of birth, place of residence, and sometimes place of birth. If the widow applied, it shows her age and the place of her residence; the date, place, and circumstances of his death; the date and place of her marriage to the veteran; and her maiden name. If the veteran left orphans, it shows their names, ages, and the places of their residence.

Related records.--An alphabetical file containing various papers relating to applicants for naval pensions includes many papers that have not yet been interfiled with the pension application files of the "Old Wars" series.

War of 1812 Series

The records.--The War of 1812 series of pension application records relates to claims based on service performed between 1812 and 1815. The records concern pensions provided for chiefly by acts approved February 14, 1871 (16 Stat. 411), and March 9, 1878 (20 Stat. 27). The former provided pensions to veterans who had served 60 days or had been cited by Congress for specific service provided they had not adhered to the Confederate cause, and to many widows of such veterans provided the marriage took place before the treaty of peace in 1815. The latter act provided for pensions to veterans who had served 14 days or in an engagement, and to widows of such veterans.

A file includes such documents as a veteran's declaration for pension, a report from the Third Auditor of the Treasury Department containing a summary of the veteran's service record, a statement showing action on the claim, and a widow's declaration for pension.

The files in the War of 1812 series are arranged alphabetically by name of veteran. Interfiled or consolidated with the files in this series are War of 1812 pension application files that had previously formed a part of the series of "Old Wars" pension application files. Likewise interfiled or consolidated with the files in this series are some War of 1812 bounty-land warrant application files from the post-Revolutionary War series described later under "Bounty-Land Warrant Application Records."

Index to the records.--The alphabetical name index is reproduced on microfilm. This index consists of a microfilm reproduction or image of the face side of each jacket (envelope) containing relevant documents. It shows the name of the veteran; the name of the widow, if any; service data; pension application and certificate numbers; and/or a bounty-land warrant application number. Certain pension application files in the War of 1812 series can be located through the use of the Remarried Widows Index, described earlier.

Information in the records.--A veteran's declaration shows the name, age, and place of residence of the veteran; if married, the maiden name of his wife; the place and date of their marriage; his rank; his military or naval unit; the date and place of his entering the service; and the date and place of his discharge. A widow's declaration shows the name, age, and place of residence of the widow; the date and place of their marriage, with the name of the official who performed the ceremony, the date and place of the veteran's death; his rank; his military or naval unit; the date and place of his entering the service; and the date and place of his discharge.

Research aid.--For identification of many pensioners of the War of 1812 and other pensioners by place of residence consult Pension Office, List of Pensioners on the Roll January 1, 1883 (47th Cong., 2d sess., S. Ex. Doc., 84; serials 2078-2082).

Related records.--Twelve record books identify by names and numbers some of the files in the War of 1812 series. Six of these books relate to claims of veterans; the other six to claims of widows of veterans. Entries are arranged alphabetically to the first three letters of the surname of the claimant.

Mexican War Series

The records.--The Mexican War series of pension application records relates to claims based on service performed 1846-48. The records are based chiefly upon an act of Congress approved January 29, 1887 (24 Stat. 371), which provided pensions for veterans who had served 60 days, or for their unremarried widows.

A file includes such documents as claims of a survivor of the Mexican War for a pension, a declaration of the widow for a pension, affidavits of witnesses, a report on service from the War or Navy Departments, a copy of the death record of the veteran, a report showing that the pensioner had been dropped from the rolls, a family data questionnaire, and, if the widow applied, a copy of the marriage record of the couple.

Consolidated with these pension application files are some Mexican War pension application files relating to death or disability incurred in service that had been formerly filed in the series of "Old Wars" pension application files, described above.

The files are arranged numerically in several subseries.

Indexes to the records.--The alphabetical name index is reproduced on microfilm. Entries in this index show the name of the veteran; the name and class of dependent, if any; service data; the application number and, for an approved claim, a pension certificate number and the State from which the claim was made. Certain pension application files in the Mexican War series can be located through the use of the Remarried Widows Index, described earlier.

Information in the records.--A veteran's declaration shows the name of the veteran; the dates and places of his birth, his enlistment, and his discharge; and the places of his residence since service. The declaration of a widow seeking a pension shows the same information about the service of the veteran; her name, age, and place of residence; the date and place of her marriage to the veteran, with the name of the person performing the ceremony; and the date and place of the death of the veteran. A filled-out questionnaire shows the maiden name of the wife; the date and place of the marriage of the couple and the name of the person performing the ceremony; the name of a former wife, if any, and the date and place of her death or divorce; and the names and dates of birth of living children.

Related records.--For Mexican War pension application files concerning men who were disabled or killed in service and in whose behalf no service claims were made, see the records in the "Old Wars" series, described above.

"Civil War and Later" Series

The records.--The "Civil War and Later series" of pension application records concerns service performed between 1861 and 1934. Excluded, however, are certain records relating to Indian wars service (described below), records relating to World War I service, and records relating to pensioners still on the rolls. Most of the records relate to Civil War service; some relate to service in the Spanish American War, the Philippine Insurrection, the Boxer Rebellion, and the Regular Establishment.

The acts under which pensions were claimed are many. Basic acts relating to Civil War service include an act approved July 14, 1862 (12 Stat. 566), which granted pensions to veterans for disability incurred in service, or to widows, children under 16, mothers, or orphan sisters under 16 of veterans whose death occurred as a result of service; an act approved January 25, 1879 (20 Stat. 265), modified by one of March 3, 1879 (20 Stat. 470), which extended benefits in connection with disability or death; an act approved June 27, 1890 (26 Stat. 182), which extended pension benefits under certain circumstances to veterans who had served 90 days or more, or to widows or other dependents; and an act approved February 6, 1907 (34 Stat. 879), which extended benefits to veterans who had served 90 days and attained the age of 62.

The number and type of documents vary greatly from file to file. They are often numerous. The documents of the greatest genealogical interest include the declaration of the veteran, the declaration of the widow, a statement of service from the War or Navy Departments, a personal history questionnaire, a family questionnaire, and a drop report.

The records are arranged in many subseries. A very few files relating to naval service of men who were killed or disabled during the Civil War are interfiled with the series of "Old Wars" pension application files. Some papers not filed in the pension application files are included in an alphabetical file relating to 19th-century naval pensioners.

Indexes to the records.--Index cards arranged alphabetically by name of veteran have been reproduced on microfilm. The reproduced cards contain the name of the veteran; the name and class of dependent, if any; service data; and the application number and, for an approved claim, the certificate number and the State from which the claim was filed.

Other index cards known as the Organization Index have also been microfilmed. These index cards contain entries relating to Army organizations that rendered service chiefly between 1861 and 1917. The cards are arranged alphabetically by name of State, thereunder numerically by regiment, thereunder alphabetically by company, and thereunder alphabetically by the veteran's name.

The award cards described later under "Pension Payment Records" identify pension application files of pensioners who were on the rolls 1907-33. Certain pension application files in the "Civil War and Later" series can be located through the use of the Remarried Widows Index described earlier.

Information in the records.--The information in the files varies depending upon the act under which the pension was applied for, the number of years of the veteran's survival after the war, and whether or not he was survived by a widow. A file contains some or all of the following information: the name, military or naval unit, and place of residence of the veteran; a summary of his military or naval record; his age or the date of his birth; place of his birth; date and place of his marriage; date and place of his death; the maiden name of his wife; the date of her death; and the names of their surviving children with the date and place of birth of each.

Use of the records.--Since the alphabetical index often shows several veterans of a particular name, it may be difficult to identify the file desired without time-consuming research. This difficulty can be resolved if the military or naval unit of the veteran is known or if the veteran was survived by a widow whose given name is known. If such facts are unknown, the problem can usually be solved if the place of residence or date of death of the veteran is known; such information appears on the award cards mentioned above.

Indian Wars Series

The records.--The Indian wars series of pension application records relate to service performed in the Indian campaigns between 1817 and 1898. An act approved July 27, 1892 (27 Stat. 281), was the first to provide service pensions for veterans of Indian wars or for their unremarried widows, but it applied only to service rendered between 1832 and 1842. Later acts extended benefits for Indian service rendered between 1817 and 1898. The number and type of documents vary greatly from file to file. The documents of the greatest genealogical interest include the declaration of the veteran, the declaration of the widow, a statement of service from the War Department, a personal history questionnaire, a family questionnaire, and a drop report. The records are arranged in several subseries and thereunder numerically.

Consolidated with these pension application files are some Indian wars pension application files that had formerly been filed in the "Old Wars" series described above.

Indexes to the records.--Index cards arranged alphabetically by name of veteran have been reproduced on microfilm. The index contains the name of the veteran; the name and class of dependent, if any; service data; and the application number and, for an approved claim, a certificate number and the State from which the claim was filed.

Certain pension application files in the Indian wars series can be located through the use of the Remarried Widows Index, described earlier.

Information in the records.--The information in the files varies depending upon the act under which the pension was applied for, the number of years of the veteran's survival after the war, and whether or not he was survived by a widow. A file contains some or all of the following information: the name, Army unit, and place of residence of the veteran; a summary of his Army record; his age or the date of his birth; the place of his birth; the date and place of his marriage; the date and place of his death; the maiden name of his wife; the date of her death; and the names of their surviving children, with the date and place of birth of each.

Use of the records.--If the index fails to reveal the name of the pensioner, a search should also be made in the "Old Wars" index or the "Civil War and Later" index, whichever is appropriate.

RECORD GROUPS

The records are in Record Group 15, Records of the Veterans Administration, except that the reports submitted to Congress on Revolutionary War invalid pensioners are in Record Group 233, Records of the United States House of Representatives, and Record Group 46, Records of the United States Senate, and the reports retained by the War Department on the same subject are in Record Group 107, Records of the Office of the Secretary of War.

PENSION PAYMENT RECORDS

The pension payment records consist of a Pension Office record book of payments to invalid pensioners, 1801-15; Pension Office record books of payments to Revolutionary War pensioners; Treasury Department records of payments to Revolutionary War and other pensioners, 1819-71; Treasury Department records of payments to naval and privateer pensioners, 1811-94; Pension Office (field) record books, 1805-1912; and Pension Office award cards, 1907-33. These records are described separately below.

Pension Office Record Book of Payments to Invalid Pensioners

The records.--The record book of payments to invalid pensioners is in one volume labeled "Revolutionary War and Acts of Military Establishment, Invalid Pensioners Payments, March 1801 through September 1815." Most of the pensioners were Revolutionary War veterans. The entries, which record semi-annual payments, are arranged by name of State and thereunder alphabetically to the first letter of the surname. The related pension application files were presumably destroyed by fire in August 1814 or before.

Information in the records.--An entry shows the name and rank of the pensioner, the name of the State in which payment was made, and the amount paid in March and September of each year. If the pensioner died or moved to another State during the period of the records, the fact is indicated, and in some cases the date of death is shown.

Research aid.--The names of the invalid pensioners in 1813 were published in War Department, Letter from the Secretary of War, Communicating a Transcript of the Pension List of the United States (Washington, 1813), copies of which are no longer available. The list has been reprinted in the Collections of the Minnesota Historical Society, vol. 6, p. 502-539 (St. Paul, 1894) and in 1959 as a publication of the Genealogical Book Co., Baltimore. It shows under the name of the State the name, rank, and amount of stipend for each pensioner in 1813.

Pension Office Record Books of Payments to Revolutionary War Pensioners

The records.--The Pension Office records of payments to Revolutionary War pensioners are in 14 unnumbered volumes, in which information is given according to certain acts of Congress approved between 1818 and 1853. The 14 volumes cover pensioners in States or Territories as follows:

Maine; New York (acts 1818-32); New York (acts 1836-53); Rhode Island, New Jersey, Delaware, District of Columbia, and Nebraska; Virginia and Tennessee; Kentucky, Missouri, and Mississippi; Massachusetts (part); Massachusetts (part) and Ohio; Pennsylvania, Maryland, and Illinois; New Hampshire and Indiana; Connecticut; Vermont and Georgia; North Carolina, South Carolina, Louisiana, Alabama, and Michigan; and Arkansas, Florida, Wisconsin, Iowa, Texas, California, Minnesota, and Oregon.

Entries are arranged by name of State or Territory of residence of the pensioner, thereunder by date of the act under which the pension was paid, and thereunder alphabetically to the first letter of the surname of the pensioner.

Information in the records.--An entry shows the name of the agency through which payment was made, the name of the pensioner, and the amount of the allowance. Many entries also show the dates of death of the pensioners.

Treasury Department Records of Payments to Revolutionary War and Other Pensioners

The Treasury Department records of payments to Revolutionary War and other pensioners include pension payment volumes, 1819-71, and final payment vouchers, 1819-64. Each type of record is described below.

Pension Payment Volumes

The records.--The pension payment volumes contain entries dated 1819-71. The 23 volumes have been microfilmed and run from letter A to letter V, with 2 volumes for letter L. Pension payments were made semiannually. Some entries record payments made in March and September each year, and other entries record payments made in June and December each year. Some entries terminate abruptly in 1820 because a number of pensioners were dropped from the rolls under terms of an act of Congress approved May 1, 1820 (3 Stat. 569). Other entries terminate because of the deaths of the pensioners.

The entries are arranged by act of Congress under which payment was made, thereunder by name of pension agency, and thereunder by the first letter of the surname of the pensioner.

Information in the records.--An entry shows the name of the pensioner, the name of the veteran, the name of the pension agency through which payment was made, and the quarter and year of the final payment. In instances in which the heirs or a legal representative claimed an unpaid balance due the pensioner, the date of death of the pensioner is given.

Use of the records.--In order to locate an entry, the following information should first be obtained from the related pension application file: the name of the veteran and, if the pensioner was the widow, the name of the widow; the date of the latest act of Congress under which payment was made; the name of the last pension agency through which payment was made; and, if there was more than one pensioner of the same name, the amount of the periodic pension payment. By consulting the typed "Key to the Pension Payment Volumes Relating to Revolutionary War Pensioners," a copy of which is in the central search room of the National Archives, a searcher may identify by volume and page the entries relating to a specific pensioner.

747-596 O - 64 - 7

Final Payment Vouchers

The records. --The final payment vouchers relate to Army pensioners who rendered Revolutionary War or later service and are dated 1819-64. Many are interfiled in a large series of vouchers that are arranged by name of State, thereunder by name of pension agency, thereunder by quarter year of payment, thereunder by date of act under which payment was made, and thereunder alphabetically to the first letter of the surname of the pensioner. Some of the final payment vouchers, however, have been consolidated with the related pension application files.

Information in the records. --Some final payment vouchers include information concerning the date and place of death of the pensioner and the names of his heirs. These vouchers will show such information if the date of death of the pensioner appears in one of the pension payment volumes described above.

Use of the records. --In requesting a final payment voucher a searcher should consult the pension application file and pertinent pension payment volumes to obtain the following information, which is needed to identify such a voucher: the name of the veteran and, if the pensioner is a widow, the name of the widow; the date of the latest act of Congress under which payment was made; the name of the last pension agency through which payment was made; the date of death of the pensioner; and the quarter year during which final payment was made.

Treasury Department Records of Payments to Naval and Privateer Pensioners

The records. --The Treasury Department records of payments to naval and privateer pensioners are dated 1815-94. They concern invalid or disabled men who served with the Navy or Marine Corps, or on privateers, chiefly between 1798 and 1865, or widows of men who died in such service. Related pension application files are, for the most part, in the "Old Wars" series or the "Civil War and Later" series of the pension application records described earlier.

The Treasury Department records include pension payment volumes and final payment vouchers. Each type of record is described below.

Pension Payment Volumes

The records. --The pension payment volumes, dated 1815-73, are folio size and record semiannual payments to pensioners in January and July of each year.

There are three volumes covering respectively the following periods: 1815-38; 1838-63, and 1846-73 (primarily 1848-66). Entries in the volumes are arranged by name of State and thereunder alphabetically to the first letter of the surname of the pensioner.

Information in the records. --An entry shows the name of the pensioner; the rank of the veteran; the date of the commencement of the pension; the amount of the monthly allowance and the quarterly or semiannual dates of payment; and, in some instances, the name of the vessel on which the person was injured or the date of his death.

Final Payment Vouchers

The records.--The final payment vouchers are dated 1815-94. They are interfiled in a large series of pension vouchers, which are arranged by name of pension agency and thereunder by date of payment. They are similar to the Revolutionary War final payment vouchers described above under "Treasury Department Records of Payments to Revolutionary War and Other Pensioners." Those dated before 1815 were presumably destroyed by fire in 1814.

Information in the records.--Some final payment vouchers show the date and place of death of the pensioner and the names of the heirs.

Use of the records.--For the period 1815-73, the vouchers can be consulted through the use of the pension payment volumes described above.

Pension Office (Field) Record Books

The records.--The Pension Office (field) record books contain entries dated 1805-1912. They record the periodic payment of pensions through the local pension agencies. The books are arranged alphabetically by the name of the city in which the last pension agency having jurisdiction over a specific area was located.

Index to the records.--The personal names entered in the volumes are unindexed, but there is a card index to the volumes. It is arranged alphabetically by the name of the city in which the pension agency was located and thereunder usually by class of pensioner. An index card contains the name of the city, the class of pensioner, the initial letters of the alphabet covered by the pensioner's surname, the period of payment covered by the volume, and the volume number. Sometimes the date of the act under which the pension payment was made appears on the card.

Information in the records.--An entry shows for each pensioner the date of death or the date of the last payment of the pension and sometimes the name of county of residence or the post office address of the pensioner.

Use of the records.--In order to use these records it is necessary to obtain from the related pension application file the name of the pensioner, the certificate number, the name of the agency through which payment was made, and the date of the final act under which payment was made.

Pension Office Award Cards

The records.--The Pension Office award cards record payments to pensioners on the rolls between 1907 and 1933 except World War I pensioners. The cards are 5" x 8" in size and are arranged alphabetically by name of pensioner.

Information in the records.--Each card shows the name of the pensioner, the name and military or naval unit of the veteran, the date of the act and the certificate number under which payment was made, and the date of the commencement of the pension. Some cards show the places of residence and dates of death of the pensioners and the names of the pension agencies from or to which jurisdiction was transferred.

Use of the records.--These cards are sometimes useful in identifying Civil War or other pension application files that cannot be identified effectively from the microfilmed indexes.

RECORD GROUPS

The records are in Record Group 15, Records of the Veterans Administration, except for the Treasury Department records of payment, which are in Record Group 217, Records of the United States General Accounting Office.

BOUNTY-LAND WARRANT APPLICATION RECORDS

A bounty-land warrant was a right to free land on the public domain. Bounty-land warrants were granted to veterans or their heirs on the basis of military service performed 1775-1855.[4]

A bounty-land warrant application file comprises the documents relating to claims for bounty land based on the service of an individual in a particular war. Such documents include an application for a warrant, a discharge certificate surrendered by the veteran or his heir to substantiate his claim, and obsolete jackets containing notations as to whether his claim was approved or disapproved.

In answer to inquiries concerning bounty-land warrant applications the National Archives from 1940 to 1950 summarized the pertinent information on typed sheets. Carbons of these sheets have been preserved and are described at the beginning of this chapter in a discussion of pension application records.

The envelope containing an approved bounty-land warrant application file is identified by a symbol that shows the number of the warrant and the number of acres granted. Most envelopes give also two numbers representing the last two digits of the year of the act under which the claim was adjudicated. The information on each envelope is sufficient to identify in the National Archives the related land-entry papers, described in a later chapter on "Land-Entry Records for the Public Land States." Since most bounty-land warrant claimants sold their rights to land, the land-entry papers seldom refer to land owned by the veteran's family unless the family moved from one of the Thirteen Original States to the public domain. Infrequently the recipient of the land warrant died before he disposed of the warrant, and the land-entry papers reveal the names of his heirs.

The envelope containing a disapproved bounty-land warrant application file is identified by a register number followed by the year of the act under which the application was submitted.

The bounty-land warrant application records form two principal series: the Revolutionary War series and the post-Revolutionary War series. These are described below. In addition, a segregated Indian series is described under "Records Concerning Indians" in the final chapter.

Revolutionary War Series

The Federal Government granted Revolutionary War bounty-land warrants on the bases of an ordinance passed by the Congress of the Confederation in 1788, an act of the Congress of the United States approved in 1855, as amended, and private acts relating to individual soldiers. The story is briefly told below.

---

[4] Congress authorized special privileges to Union veterans of the Civil War who applied for homesteads but did not authorize the granting of bounty-land warrants.

On September 16, 1776, Congress passed a resolution (*Journals of the Continental Congress*, vol. 5, p. 762-763) promising free land in the public domain to officers and soldiers who engaged in service and continued to serve during the Revolutionary War and to representatives of such officers and soldiers as were slain by the enemy. This resolution, as amended, provided that each private or noncommissioned officer was entitled to 100 acres, each lieutenant 200 acres, and so on, the highest amount being 1,100 acres for a major general. The resolution was implemented by an ordinance passed by the Congress of the Confederation on July 9, 1788 (*Journals of the Continental Congress*, vol. 34, p. 307-308), which authorized the Secretary at War to issue land warrants based on such service.

An act of March 3, 1803 (2 Stat. 236), was the first of many acts to provide warrants for soldiers who had not perfected their claims within time limits previously authorized.

An act of Congress approved March 3, 1855 (10 Stat. 701), extended bounty-land warrant benefits and provided for warrants for 160 acres of land on the basis of 14 days' service or service in a battle. This resulted in applications in behalf of many additional soldiers and their heirs and in behalf of soldiers and their heirs who had been entitled to only 100 acres under previous law. Section 4 of an act of Congress approved May 14, 1856 (11 Stat. 8), provided similar benefits to Revolutionary War naval servicemen and their heirs.

Most Revolutionary War warrants issued on the basis of acts before 1855 were converted into tracts of land in the United States Military District of Ohio, but by 1830 warrant owners were able to exchange warrants for scrip and obtain other land in the public domain. The many Revolutionary War bounty-land warrants converted into tracts of land in the Virginia Military District of Ohio were based upon Virginia warrants rather than upon Federal warrants. These records are described in the chapter on "Land-Entry Records for the Public Land States."

The records.--The bounty-land warrant application records concern warrants issued 1789-1800 and under the act of 1803 and later acts.

The application files relating to over 14,000 numbered warrants issued 1789-1800 under authority of the ordinance passed in 1788 have been presumably destroyed by fire. Record books identifying the destroyed application files, however, have been preserved and are described under "Related records," below. Each entry concerning a destroyed file has been transcribed on a large record card.

The application files relating to the warrants issued under authority of the act of 1803 and later acts are extant. The warrants are consecutively numbered beginning with 1, except for the warrants issued under the acts of 1855 and 1856, which are numbered in a sequence of numbers that relates also to post-Revolutionary War warrants. A file includes such documents as the application of the veteran or his heir, an assignment of rights to the warrant, a discharge certificate surrendered as evidence of service, and an obsolete jacket containing evidence of action on the claim.

The extant files and the record cards used as substitutes for the missing files are arranged alphabetically and interfiled in the Revolutionary War service series described earlier under "Pension Application Records."

Indexes to the records.--The indexes described earlier for the Revolutionary War service series of pension application files also contain entries for the files of veterans on whose service claims for bounty land were based, except for veterans whose surnames begin A-Del.

Information in the records.--A file contains such information as the name, age, residence, military or naval unit, and period of service of the veteran; and the name, age, and place of residence of the widow or other claimant. If the application was approved, the file shows also the warrant number, the number of acres granted, the date issued, and, where appropriate, the name of the assignee.

If the file was destroyed, the card used as a stubstitute shows the name of the veteran, his grade, his military or naval unit, the warrant number, the number of acres granted, the date issued, and, where appropriate, the name of the assignee.

Related records.--Pension Office record books relating solely to Federal Revolutionary War bounty-land warrants are divided into an old series and a new series. The old series, relating to claims filed 1789-1800, is in five volumes. Volume 1 relates chiefly to officers with warrant Nos. 1-2716. Volumes 2-4 relate chiefly to soldiers as follows: volume 2 for New Hampshire, Rhode Island, Massachusetts, and Connecticut (part), Nos. 2901-6162; volume 3 for Pennsylvania, Delaware, Connecticut (continued), New York, and New Jersey, Nos. 6163-10918; and volume 4 for Maryland, Virginia, and miscellaneous, Nos. 10919-14757. Volume 5 duplicates the entries in volume 1 except that the entries are arranged alphabetically to the first letter of the surname. The related bounty-land warrant application files are not extant, but the individual entries have been transcribed on large record cards, which are interfiled as noted above.

The new series is in one volume that lists and identifies in alphabetical order to the first letter of the surname all other veterans in whose behalf Federal Revolutionary War warrants were claimed except those claiming under the acts of 1855 and 1856, cited above. The related bounty-land warrant applications files are extant and have been described above.

Post-Revolutionary War Series

Congress passed numerous acts providing bounty-land benefits for veterans who served after the Revolutionary War and for their heirs. The most liberal and last was the act approved March 3, 1855 (10 Stat. 702), which authorized the issuance of bounty-land warrants for 160 acres of land provided that the veteran had served 14 days or in a battle. These benefits extended to wagonmasters and teamsters employed in time of war in the transportation of military stores and supplies.

The first acts providing for warrants issued on the basis of War of 1812 service limited the location of the warrants to military reservations established in Arkansas, Illinois, or Missouri. Unused warrants could later be exchanged for tracts elsewhere in the public domain.

The records.--The post-Revolutionary War series of bounty-land warrant application files relates only to service performed between 1790 and 1855, chiefly in the War of 1812, the Indian wars, and the Mexican War.

A file contains such documents as the application of the veteran or his widow, a discharge certificate surrendered as evidence of service, and an obsolete jacket indicating action on the claim.

The files are arranged alphabetically by name of veteran, except that some War of 1812 files have been interfiled or consolidated with the War of 1812 series of pension application files described above under "Pension Application Records."

Index to the records.--The index described earlier for the War of 1812 pension application files also contains entries for some of the files of veterans on whose service claims for bounty land were based.

Information in the records.--A file shows such information as the name, age, residence, rank, military or naval unit, and period of service of the veteran, and sometimes his personal description. If the applicant was an heir it shows such information as the date and place of death of the veteran, the name of the heir or heirs, and the degree of relationship. If the application was approved it also shows the number of the warrant, the number of acres granted, and the year of the act under which the warrant was granted.

RECORD GROUPS

The records are in Record Group 15, Records of the Veterans Administration.

CLAIMS FILES FOR SPECIAL NAVAL AWARDS

The claims files for special naval awards relate chiefly to claims for prize money. Although naval servicemen were in some instances entitled to bounty-land warrants, their principal benefit in addition to their pay was prize money awarded on the basis of prizes captured on the high seas during time of war. These claims files are interfiled with Treasury Department payment records in the large "Miscellaneous Account" file. For a description of the portion of the files that relates to prize money, see Edward H. West, "Applications for Prize Money," in National Genealogical Society Quarterly, 32: 65-68.

The segregable series of claims for special naval awards include half-pay files of Virginia naval officers of the Revolutionary War and claims of the heirs of men lost at sea. Each type of record is described below.

Half-Pay Files of Virginia Naval Officers of the Revolutionary War

The records.--The half-pay files of Virginia naval officers of the Revolutionary War, 1832-59, are based upon an act of Congress approved July 5, 1832 (4 Stat. 563). By this act Congress assumed the responsibility of awarding to Virginia naval officers sums equal to one-half their pay from the termination of their Revolutionary War service until their deaths. These awards had been agreed to by a Virginia resolution of May 1779.

The papers relating to each claim are arranged in a separate file, and the files are arranged alphabetically by name of veteran. There is an appropriate cross reference to each file in the Revolutionary War service series of pension application files; and each file is further identified in the "Index of Revolutionary War Pension Applications" in the March 1943 and later issues of the National Genealogical Society Quarterly.

Information in the records.--Each file contains the same type of information as in a Revolutionary War pension application file, except that there is often much more information about the identification of the heirs.

Claims of the Heirs of Men Lost at Sea

In certain cases special funds have been put aside to satisfy claims of the heirs of men lost at sea. The records relating to such claims include records relating to the U. S. brig *Epervier* and records relating to the U. S. schooner *Grampus*.

Records Relating to the U. S. Brig "Epervier"

The records.--The claims of the heirs of the men lost on the U. S. brig *Epervier* were based upon an act of Congress approved March 3, 1817 (3 Stat. 369). This act provided for the heirs the equivalent of 6 months' pay in addition to the pay due the deceased on July 14, 1815.

The documents relating to a claim include a receipt acknowledging payment by the agent, Benjamin Homans, a copy of the marriage record of the deceased or an affidavit identifying his orphans, power of attorney, and related correspondence.

The claims are arranged in two large envelopes alphabetically by name of naval serviceman.

Information in the records.--A claim shows such information as the maiden name of the wife of the naval serviceman, the date and place of their marriage, and the place of her residence or the identification of orphans or other heirs.

Records Relating to the U. S. Schooner "Grampus"

The records.--The claims of the heirs of the men lost on the U. S. schooner *Grampus* are dated 1843-45. The claims were made on the basis of a fund raised for the relief of the heirs.

The documents in a claims file include receipts, a copy of the marriage record, the application, and correspondence. The claims are arranged alphabetically in two large envelopes.

Information in the records.--A claims file shows the maiden name of the wife of the naval serviceman, the date and place of her marriage to him, and the place of her residence or the identification of orphans or other heirs by name and place of residence and dates of birth.

RECORD GROUP

The records are in Record Group 15, Records of the Veterans Administration.

RECORDS OF FEDERAL HOMES

The records of Federal homes in the National Archives are dated 1851-1935, with some as late as 1942. They relate to veterans who had served in the armed forces of the United States and who spent at least some time during their advanced years in Federal homes. They include records of the National Home for Disabled Volunteer Soldiers and its successor agency, the Veterans Administration, and records of the United States Soldiers' Home. These records are described separately below.

Records of the National Home for Disabled Volunteer Soldiers

The National Home for Disabled Volunteer Soldiers was created under provisions of an act of Congress approved March 21, 1866 (14 Stat. 10). In 1930 it was consolidated with certain other agencies to form the Veterans Administration.

Following is a list of the branches of the Home together with their location and the years of their creation:

Eastern Branch, Togus, near Augusta, Maine, 1866
Central Branch, Dayton, Ohio, 1867
Northwestern Branch, Wood, near Milwaukee, Wis., 1867
Southern Branch, Kecoughtan, near Hampton, Va., 1870
Western Branch, Leavenworth, Kans., 1884
Pacific Branch, Sawtelle, near Los Angeles, Calif., 1888
Marion Branch, Marion, Ind., 1888
Danville Branch, Danville, Ill., 1898
Mountain Branch, Mountain Home, near Johnson City, Tenn., 1903
Battle Mountain Sanitarium, Hot Springs, S. Dak., 1907
Bath Branch, Bath, N. Y., 1929, successor to the New York State Home at Bath, 1878

The Home admitted disabled officers, soldiers, sailors, and marines who had been honorably discharged and who had served in the regular, volunteer, or other forces of the United States.

The records of the National Home for Disabled Volunteer Soldiers are dated 1866-1934. They include (1) historical registers and (2) registers of deaths at the New York State Home at Bath(later the Bath Branch). Each kind of register is described below.

Historical Registers

The records.--The historical registers are folio-size volumes in separate series. There is a series relating to each branch of the Home cited above, including the former New York State Home at Bath. Entries in a series date from the formation of the branch to or about 1934. Each page in each register is devoted exclusively to the history of one veteran. Entries are arranged numerically by register number.

Indexes to the records.--For each branch there is at least one separate series of bound volumes of indexes. Entries are usually arranged alphabetically to the second or third letter of the surname and include the veteran's register number.

Information in the records.--An entry gives the following information about the veteran: name; date on which he was admitted to the branch; service rendered in the armed forces of the United States; place of birth; age; personal description; religion; occupation; place of former residence; marital status; name and address of his next-of-kin; and, if he was a member of the branch at the time of his death, the date of death. If the veteran was buried in the branch cemetery, the location of the grave is given.

Related information.--For information about burials of veterans at branches of the Home, see "Application for headstones" under "Burial Records of Soldiers" in the chapter on "United States Military Records."

Registers of Deaths at the Former New York State Home at Bath

The records.--The registers of deaths at the former New York State Home at Bath are dated 1879-1929. Entries are arranged chronologically in three volumes, each of which has an index to the first letter of the surname.

Information in the records.--An entry contains the following information about the veteran: name; service rendered in the armed forces of the United States; place of birth; age; date and place of death; and place of burial. If the place of burial was in the Home cemetery, the grave number is given. An entry may include the name and address of the relative notified of the death.

Records of the United States Soldiers' Home

The United States Soldiers' Home, originally named the Military Asylum, was created under terms of an act of Congress approved March 3, 1851 (9 Stat. 595). It is chiefly a Home for veterans of the Regular Army.

Accessioned records of the United States Soldiers' Home are dated 1851-1942. They include registers of inmates, a register of deaths, and copies of certificates of death. Each kind of record is described separately below.

Registers of Inmates

The records.--The registers of inmates are in four folio-size volumes and cover the following years: volume 1, 1851-78 (old volume); volume 2, 1851-87; volume 3, 1888-1907; and volume 4, 1907-8. The entries are alphabetized to the first letter of the surname.

Information in the records.--An entry includes, in addition to the name and date of admission of the veteran, such information as the place of his birth, the number of years of his service, the nature of his infirmities, the place of residence of his family, and sometimes the date of his death. The information in volume 1 is partially duplicated in volume 2; but an entry in volume 1 also gives a personal description of the veteran and his military history.

Register of Deaths

The records.--The register of deaths at Barnes Hospital, United States Soldiers' Home, consists of one unindexed volume, with entries dated 1852-1942. Entries are numbered and arranged chronologically.

Information in the records.--Each entry shows the name of the veteran, the date of death, military unit, age, date and place of birth, and the cause of death.

Copies of Certificates of Death

The records.--The copies of certificates of death are District of Columbia forms dated 1876-89 and 1913-29. They are arranged chronologically and are unindexed.

Information in the records. -- Each entry shows such information as the name of the veteran, his age or the date of his birth, the place of birth, the date of death, the place of burial, and the name of the undertaker.

RECORD GROUPS

The records of the National Home for Disabled Volunteer Soldiers are in Record Group 15, Records of the Veterans Administration. The records of the United States Soldiers' Home are in Record Group 231, Records of the United States Soldiers' Home.

VI. RECORDS CONCERNING THE CONFEDERATE STATES OF AMERICA

The National Archives has many records concerning the Confederate States of America. They include compiled military service records; records relating to naval and marine personnel; citizens files; amnesty and pardon records; and cotton bills of sale. Each kind of record is described separately below.

COMPILED MILITARY SERVICE RECORDS

The records.--The compiled military service records consist of 3-1/4" x 8" cards on which the U. S. War Department, between 1903 and 1927, abstracted information on officers, noncommissioned officers, and enlisted men from Union prison and parole records and from captured and other surviving Confederate records, such as muster rolls, returns, rosters, payrolls, appointment books, and hospital registers. All the cards relating to the same soldier are filed together in one jacket-envelope. Filed in this envelope are also originals of any papers that relate solely to the particular soldier.

The abstracts made from the original records were verified by a separate operation of comparison, and every conceivable precaution was taken to ensure that the abstracts were accurate.

Most of the compiled military service records are arranged alphabetically by name of State; thereunder by branch of service such as cavalry, artillery, or infantry; thereunder by organization; and thereunder by personal name. There are also, however, two other series. One consists of jacket-envelopes for men who served in military units raised directly by the Confederate Government (such as the 1st Confederate Infantry, Morgan's Calvary, and the Cherokee Mounted Rifles), arranged by organization and thereunder alphabetically by personal name. The other series consists of jacket-envelopes known as the General and Staff Officers' Papers, which include records not only for officers occupying staff positions but also for noncommissioned officers and enlisted men performing staff services; these records are arranged alphabetically by personal name.

All the compiled service records that are arranged by State or Territory have been microfilmed. The States are Alabama, Arkansas, Florida, Georgia, Kentucky, Louisiana, Maryland, Mississippi, Missouri, North Carolina, South Carolina, Tennessee, Texas, and Virginia; and the Territory of Arizona. The other two series have also been microfilmed.

Indexes to the records.--The indexes are on 3-1/4" x 8" cards, arranged alphabetically by name of soldier and showing the unit in which he served. One is a consolidated index, which refers both to the records for the individual States and the records in the two other series. This index has been microfilmed. There is also a separate index to the compiled service records of soldiers belonging to units from each of the following States: Alabama, Arkansas, Florida, Georgia, Kentucky, Louisiana, Maryland,

Mississippi, Missouri, North Carolina, South Carolina, Tennessee, Texas, and Virginia; and the Territory of Arizona. They have all been microfilmed.

Unless the unit in which a soldier served is already known, his compiled service record can be readily located only through the use of one of these indexes.

Information in the records.--A jacket-envelope shows the name of the soldier, the name of the State from which he served, the name of his company and regiment, and his rank. The cards and papers in the envelope show other information, such as the dates of changes in the soldier's rank, the date and place of his enlistment and discharge, his occupation, and his personal description. If the soldier was captured, they may show the date of his death, if it occurred in camp, or the date of his release and parole. References to the original records are included on the cards.

Research aids.--Some Confederate soldiers are named in War Department, The War of the Rebellion: a Compilation of the Official Records of the Union and Confederate Armies (Washington, 1880-1901). The last volume is a general index. This voluminous publication, including the index, has been microfilmed.

Information about the confirmation of appointments of Confederate officers is given in Confedederate States of America, Congress, Journal of the Congress of the Confederate States of America, 1861-65 (58th Cong., 2d sess., S. Doc. 234; serials 4610-4616). A general index is in the last volume.

Perhaps the most genealogically useful printed roster of soldiers of a Confederate State is the following indexed publication: Louisiana, Commissioner of Military Records, Records of Louisiana Confederate Soldiers and Louisiana Confederate Commands . . . Compiled by Andrew B. Booth, Commissioner, Louisiana Military Records (New Orleans, 1920).

RECORDS RELATING TO NAVAL AND MARINE PERSONNEL

The records relating to naval and marine personnel of the Confederate States of America in the National Archives include compiled hospital and prison records, reference cards and papers, shipping articles, and muster rolls. Each type of record is described below.

Compiled Hospital and Prison Records

The records.--These records consist of cards on which the U. S. War Department, when it was compiling the military service records, abstracted information on naval and marine personnel from Union and Confederate hospital registers, prescription books, and other records and from Union prison and parole rolls. Filed with these are the originals of papers, primarily from prison records, relating to the individual. The records are arranged alphabetically by name of sailor or marine. They have been microfilmed.

Information in the records.--The cards and papers show the name of the person and his ship or station and such other information as the date and place of capture, release, or parole, and place of confinement; and the date, place, and cause of admission to a hospital and the date of discharge. References to the original records are included on the cards.

Reference Cards and Papers

The records.--These records, which are known to be incomplete, consist of cards prepared by the U. S. War Department, probably in the latter part of the 19th century, showing references to vessel papers, payrolls, muster rolls, and other documents relating to service in the Confederate Navy and Marine Corps. Filed with them sometimes are original documents relating solely to the particular person. The records are in two series, one for naval personnel and one for marine personnel, and they are arranged alphabetically by surname in each series. They have been microfilmed.

Information in the records.--The records show the name and rank of the sailor or marine and are a possible means of finding other information about his service.

Shipping Articles

The records.--The National Archives has a few shipping articles for enlisted men in the Confederate States Navy, 1861-65. They are bound in one volume, which contains a typed index.

Information in the records.--An entry on the shipping articles shows the name of the enlisted man, his rating, his signature, and the date of his enlistment.

Muster Rolls and Payrolls

The records.--The National Archives has some muster rolls and payrolls of vessels and marine detachments of the Confederate States Navy. They are sheets and booklets in wrappers labeled by name of vessel or marine detachment. They are unindexed.

Information in the records.--An entry in the rolls shows the name and rank of the naval serviceman or marine.

Research aids.--For identification of Confederate naval officers consult Office of Naval Records and Library, Register of Officers of the Confederate States Navy, 1861-65 (Washington, 1931). Names in it are arranged alphabetically.

Some Confederate naval servicemen and marines are named in Navy Department, Official Records of the Union and Confederate Navies in the War of the Rebellion, General Index (69th Cong., 1st sess., H. Doc. 113; serial 8603). This consists in part of a personal name index to 30 volumes of transcripts of official and other records.

CITIZENS FILES

The citizens files relate chiefly to civilians of the Southern States during and shortly after the Civil War. They consist of the Confederate citizens file and the Union citizens file. Each is described below.

Confederate "Citizens File"

The records.--The Confederate citizens file, 1861-65, comprises papers of the Confederate States of America relating to many thousands of citizens. Typical documents are receipted bills and vouchers for service and supplies requisitioned from individuals by the Confederate Government and papers relating to claims against the Government for damages. The file also includes cross-references to pages of bound volumes of Confederate records. Documents are arranged alphabetically by name of person or firm. These records have been microfilmed.

Information in the records. --A document shows such information as the name of a citizen, the place of his residence, and the date and nature of his transaction with the Confederate Government.

"Union Provost Marshal Citizens File"

The records. --This file, 1861-67, consists of a miscellany of correspondence, reports, affidavits, loyalty oaths, lists, and other papers of Union provost marshals relating to civilians suspected of anti-Union sentiments or activities, those violating military orders, those claiming pay for property used or taken by the Union military authorities or for supplies or services furnished the Army, civilian prisoners and some military prisoners, and persons authorized to travel in or enter the Confederate States. Most of the postwar papers concern freedmen and whites in the Southern States. Many documents dated 1861-66 are arranged alphabetically by name of person. Other documents of the same dates are arranged numerically because they contain the names of more than one person, but cross-references have been prepared in the alphabetically arranged file. These records have been microfilmed. The documents for 1867 are in a separate group.

Information in the records. --The records show such information as the name and place of residence of a person, together with a varying amount of information depending upon the circumstances in the case.

AMNESTY AND PARDON RECORDS

The amnesty and pardon records, 1863-67, are based upon proclamations authorized under section 13 of an act of Congress approved July 17, 1862 (12 Stat. 592). They include amnesty oaths and amnesty papers. Each kind of record is described below.

Amnesty Oaths

The records. --The series of amnesty oaths, 1863-67, relate to a vast number of Southern people who wished to gain or regain U. S. citizenship. Usually the oath, a single document, is all that relates to one person. Filed with the oaths, in appropriate instances, are acknowledgements of warrants of Presidential pardons and agreements to accept conditions of pardon. Documents relating to one person are arranged by name of State, thereunder usually alphabetically to the first two letters of the surname. Documents relating to more than one person are arranged numerically, usually under the name of State. Some of the latter are in a miscellaneous group. Names on documents relating to more than one person are cross-referenced in the series of documents relating to one person.

Information in the records. --An oath shows the name of the person; the place the oath was taken, which was often the place of his residence; the date the oath was taken; and usually the signature of the person taking the oath. Some oaths give the ages and personal descriptions of persons taking the oaths and, in appropriate instances, the identifications of their Confederate military organizations.

Use of the records. --As many of the oaths show places of residence and as, for many persons, the places of residence were the same in 1860 and 1870, an effective search of the amnesty oaths may serve to direct a search in the population census schedules to those for the proper county.

Amnesty Papers

The records. --The series of amnesty papers, chiefly 1865-67, consists of applications for Presidential pardons on the part of persons belonging to classes listed in the proclamation of May 29, 1865 (13 Stat. 758). Among these classes were former high Confederate officials and persons owning $20,000 worth of property or more. The application files, which include supporting documents, are arranged by name of State, thereunder alphabetically by name of applicant.

Information in the records. --An application file gives the name, age, occupation, and place of residence of the applicant, together with autobiographical data.

COTTON SALE RECORDS

The records. --Cotton bills of sale, vouchers, and registers and lists of cotton sales, 1862-65, show transactions between individual cotton sellers and the Confederate States of America. They are arranged by State. Discrete series of cotton bills of sale are available for Alabama and Mississippi only; these are arranged numerically and by county, respectively.

Indexes to the records. --There are various indexes in volume form to these records.

Information in the records. --Each entry shows the name of the cotton seller, the name of the county or parish in the State where the sale occurred, the number of bales of cotton sold, the value in Confederate currency or bonds, and the date of sale.

Research aid. --The information in the records is transcribed in Treasury Department, Cotton Sold to the Confederate States (62d Cong., 3d sess., S. Doc. 987; serial 6348). The entries are arranged by name of seller in two alphabetical sequences, one for sellers in Alabama, Arkansas, Florida, Georgia, Louisiana, Mississippi, and South Carolina, and one for sellers who sold through the Texas Cotton Bureau at Houston.

GENERAL OBSERVATIONS

Related Records

For information about pensions applied for on the basis of Confederate military, naval, or marine service, address the appropriate archival or other depository at the State capital of the State for which service was rendered or in which the veteran resided after service.

Record Groups

The records are in Record Group 109, War Department Collection of Confederate Records, except that the navy shipping articles and the muster rolls and payrolls are in Record Group 45, Naval Records Collection of the Office of Naval Records and Library; amnesty oaths are in Record Group 59, General Records of the Department of State; amnesty papers are in Record Group 94, Records of the Adjutant General's Office; and cotton bills of sale are in Record Group 56, General Records of the Department of the Treasury.

747-596 O - 64 - 8

VII. LAND-ENTRY RECORDS FOR THE PUBLIC-LAND STATES

The land records in the National Archives consist principally[1] of land-entry records for the public-land States. They are dated chiefly 1800-1950, but some concern earlier transactions, a few as early as 1685. The land-entry records consist of documents that relate to rights or claims to land before grants or "patents" were issued by the Federal Government. Any personal information of genealogical value that may be found in these records before the passage of the Homestead Act in 1862 is merely incidental to the General Land Office's basic function of land disposal. Genealogical data appearing in land records before 1862, with the exception of certain private land claims, donation entry files for Florida, Washington, and Oregon, and Revolutionary bounty-land scrip applications, are usually limited to the name of the entryman and the place of residence he gave at the time he made his purchase or entry. This "place of residence" is seldom the name of the city or State from which he came originally or from which he may have moved prior to buying the land.

The public-land States are Alabama, Alaska, Arizona, Arkansas, California, Colorado, Florida, Idaho, Illinois, Indiana, Iowa, Kansas, Louisiana, Michigan, Minnesota, Mississippi, Missouri, Montana, Nebraska, Nevada, New Mexico, North Dakota, Ohio, Oklahoma, Oregon, South Dakota, Utah, Washington, Wisconsin, and Wyoming.

A person could obtain title to a tract only after it had been surveyed. With the exception of surveys in a portion of Ohio,[2] the surveys follow a uniform pattern. The surveys depend upon east and west base lines and north and south meridians. Parallel to the meridians are ranges of townships. Each township is 6 miles square and consists of 36 numbered sections. A section consists of 640 acres and is divided into 4 quarter sections of 160 acres each. A tract is normally described in terms of quarter section, section, township, and range: for example, northeast quarter of section 15, township 2 north, range 8 east of the sixth principal meridian.[3] After an individual obtained a certificate of title or its equivalent he was issued a patent. Copies of these patents are in patent books in the Bureau of Land Management, Washington 25, D. C.

---

[1]The National Archives has abstracts of title to tracts of land not originally owned but later acquired by the Federal Government, such as the Gettysburg National Military Park or the Baltimore Customs Office. The National Archives also has a list of North Carolina land grants in Tennessee, 1778-91, which has been microfilmed.

[2]For surveys of Ohio lands, see William E. Peters, Ohio Lands and Their Subdivision (Athens, Ohio, 1918).

[3]For information about the system of identifying individual tracts see plate 87, James Truslow Adams and R. V. Coleman, ed., Atlas of American History (New York, 1943).

Under provisions of the land ordinance approved May 20, 1785 (Journals of the Continental Congress, vol. 28, p. 375-381), land in the public domain was to be sold by the National Government through the loan offices of the Board of Treasury. The first such land, located in areas included in present Ohio, was sold in 1787. Information about the sales and about the location of related records appears in Albion Morris Dyer, First Ownership of Ohio Lands (Boston, 1911), reprinted from volumes 64 and 65 of the New England Historical and Genealogical Register. This publication lists also the names of the original French proprietors of Gallipolis who received lands by acts of Congress, 1795-98.

The land-entry records in the National Archives include records relating to entries based on purchases or special conditions of settlement, 1800-June 30, 1908; bounty-land warrant records, chiefly 1789-June 30, 1908; private land claims records, chiefly 1789-June 30, 1908; and the numerical series, July 1, 1908-December 31, 1950. Each kind of record is described separately.

RECORDS RELATING TO ENTRIES BASED ON PURCHASES OR SPECIAL CONDITIONS OF SETTLEMENT, 1800-JUNE 30, 1908

Pursuant to an act of Congress approved May 10, 1800 (2 Stat. 73), four district land offices were established in that portion of the Northwest Territory that became Ohio. Gradually other land offices were set up throughout the public domain. These land offices were responsible for handling requests for land. Each file of documents relating to a request for land was transmitted to Washington after the file had been completed or the request abandoned. The documents based on purchases or special conditions of settlement were arranged by State, thereunder by name of land office, thereunder by series, and thereunder numerically. A list of the land offices together with the principal series for each land office is given in National Archives, Preliminary Inventory of the Land-Entry Papers of the General Land Office (Washington, 1949).

The records are of several kinds. Those of genealogical interest include credit entry files, cash entry files, donation entry files, and homestead entry files. Each kind is described below.

Credit Entry Files

Nearly all the land sold by the Federal Government between 1800 and June 30, 1820, was sold on credit through the few land offices then in operation at no less than $2.00 an acre in accordance with the terms of an act of Congress approved May 10, 1800 (2 Stat. 73). Sale of land on credit was discontinued after June 30, 1820, but many purchasers of land previously bought on credit on which installments were overdue were enabled to obtain title to their tracts on the basis of relief acts beginning with an act of Congress approved March 2, 1821 (3 Stat. 612).

The records.--Of genealogical interest in the credit entry files are what are called "credit entry final certificates," 1800-1835 and later, which were issued on the basis of completed purchases. Occasionally a document such as an assignment was filed with the final certificate. Credit entry certificates are filed among the papers of each appropriate land office in two numerical series. One is for certificates issued prior to July 1, 1820, "credit prior certificates;" the other is for certificates issued under relief legislation, "credit under certificates." Normally, the receipts for purchases are not filed with the related final certificates but are in separate series.

Indexes to the records.--The Bureau of Land Management, Washington 25, D. C., has five volumes of indexes to Ohio tract books relating to the years 1800-1820 and later. The books are for the following land offices: Canton (Wooster); Chillicothe; Cincinnati; Marietta and Zanesville; and Steubenville. Entries in the indexes are arranged alphabetically to the first letter of the surname. From the description of the tracts in the tract books in the Bureau of Land Management it is possible to locate the related entry file in the National Archives.

Information in the records.--A final certificate normally shows the name and place of residence of the entryman as given at the time of purchase; the date of the purchase; the number of acres in the tract; the description of the tract in terms of subdivision, section, township, and range; a summary of the payments made; and a citation to the record copy of the patent in the Bureau of Land Management.

Cash Entry Files

Nearly all the land sold by the Federal Government to individual settlers on and after July 1, 1820, was sold for cash at no less than $1.25 an acre, pursuant to an act approved April 24, 1820 (3 Stat. 566).

The records.--The cash entry files, which are arranged by name of land office, are dated 1820-June 30, 1908, but the series for a specific land office cover usually only a part of this period. A file includes the application for the tract, the receipt for monies paid, and a final certificate authorizing the claimant to obtain a patent. If the tract paid for was claimed on the basis of a preemption claim, the file may include a preemption proof or similar document. If the tract paid for was entered as a homestead and the homestead entry had been commuted to a cash entry, the cash entry file includes the homestead entry file.

Index to the records.--A master index to the cash entry files for Alabama, Alaska, Arizona, Florida, Louisiana, Nevada, and Utah is on 3" x 5" cards.

Information in the records.--Each final certificate shows the name of the entryman; the place of his residence given at the time of purchase; the description of the tract in terms of subdivision, section, township, and range; the number of acres in the tract; the date of the patent; and the volume and page of the record copy of the patent in the Bureau of Land Management, Washington 25, D. C. The testimony of claimant in a preemption proof shows the name of the claimant, his age, his citizenship, the date of his entry on the tract, the number and relationship of members of his household, and the nature of the improvements on the tract. The information in a homestead entry file is given below under "Homestead Entry Files."

Donation Entry Files

The donation entry files concern land given away in return for certain conditions of settlement. They include Florida donation entry files and Oregon and Washington donation entry files, described separately below.

Florida Donation Entry Files

Under terms of the Florida Armed Occupation Act approved August 4, 1842 (5 Stat. 502), as amended, men able to bear arms were entitled to apply for 160 acres of land in certain unsettled areas of East Florida and were given patents to the land upon fulfilling the condition of 5 years' settlement.

The records.--The Florida donation entry files, mainly 1842-50, for each appropriate land office are filed in a single numerical series. The documents in each file vary depending upon the extent to which title had been perfected. A complete file contains a permit to settle, an application for a patent, a report by the land agent, and a final certificate authorizing the claimant to obtain a patent.

Index to the records.--An index to the files that include final certificates is on 3" x 5" cards as part of a master card index.

Information in the records.--A permit to settle shows the name of the applicant, his marital status, the month and year he became a resident of Florida, and a description of the land in terms of subdivision, section, township, and range. An application for a patent shows the name of the applicant, a description of the land, the name of the settler, and the period of his settlement. A final certificate shows the name of the applicant, a description of the land, the date of the patent, and the volume and page number of the recorded copy of the patent in the Bureau of Land Management, Washington 25, D. C.

Oregon and Washington Donation Files

Under terms of an act of Congress approved September 27, 1850 (9 Stat. 496), certain white settlers and half-breed Indians in Oregon Territory and certain settlers arriving there between December 1, 1850, and December 1, 1853, were entitled to land. The number of acres granted depended upon the marital status of the settler and the date of settlement, and it varied from 160 to 640. Settlers were required to reside on the land and clutivate it for 4 years.

The records.--The Oregon and Washington donation files for each appropriate land office are filed in two numerical series. One relates to complete entries, the other to incomplete entries. A file relating to a complete entry includes the notification on the settlement of public land and the donation certificate.

Indexes to the records.--A one-volume index to registers of the Oregon donation claims and another such index to registers of the Washington donation claims contain entries to the first letter of the surname. A third one-volume index is an index to the registers of both the Oregon donation claims and the Washington donation claims, but it contains some gaps. The registers fully identify each claim.

The National Archives also has a roll of microfilm prepared by the Oregon State Library that lists alphabetically the Oregon donation claims and identifies each. This information was printed serially by the Genealogical Forum of Portland, Oreg., under the title "Index to Oregon Donation Land Claims." Each index gives the name of the entryman, name of the land office, certificate number, number of acres, township, range, and section of each approved claim.

Information in the records.--A notification on the settlement of public land shows the description of the land in terms of subdivision, section, township, and range; the name of the entryman; the place of his residence at the time of notification; his citizenship; the date and place of his birth; and, if married, the given name of his wife and the date and place of their marriage. A donation certificate shows the name of the entryman, the place of his residence, the description of the land, the date of the patent, and the volume and page number of the recorded copy in the Bureau of Land Management, Washington 25, D. C.

Homestead Entry Files

Under the Homestead Act approved May 20, 1862 (12 Stat. 392), citizens and persons who had filed their intentions to become citizens were given 160 acres of land in the public domain if they fulfilled certain conditions. In general, an applicant had to build a home on the land, reside there for 5 years, and cultivate the land. Some later acts modified or waived some of these conditions. An act approved June 8, 1872 (17 Stat. 333), for example, provided special benefits for Union veterans or their widows and orphans.

The records.--The homestead entry papers filed by name of land office are dated 1863-June 30, 1908. Usually there are two separately numbered series for each land office, one relating to complete homestead entries and the other relating to incomplete homestead entries. A complete homestead entry file includes such documents as the homestead application, the certificate of publication of intention to make a claim, the homestead proof consisting of testimonies of two witnesses and the testimony of the claimant, and the final certificate authorizing the claimant to obtain a patent; and also, when appropriate, a copy of naturalization proceedings or a copy of a Union veteran's discharge certificate. The photoduplication of naturalization proceedings is restricted by law.

Information in the records.--A homestead application shows the name of the entryman, the place of his residence at the time of application, the description of the tract, and the number of acres in the tract. The testimony of claimant on a homestead proof shows a description of the tract; the name, age, and post office address of the claimant; a description of the house and the date when residence was established therein; the number and relationship of members of the family; the nature of the crops; and the number of acres under cultivation. A final certificate shows the location of the tract, the name and post office address of the claimant, the date the patent was issued, and the volume and page number of the recorded copy of the patent in the Bureau of Land Management Washington 25, D. C. A copy of naturalization proceedings relating to a naturalized citizen or an alien who had declared his intention of becoming a citizen shows such information as the name of the immigrant, the date and port of his arrival, and the place of his birth.

Related records.--Some entrymen who applied for homesteads wanted to obtain possession of the tracts before the passage of the time required by law. Such persons purchased the tracts for cash at the established price instead of fulfilling the homestead conditions. The homestead entry files in such cases are filed with the cash entry files pertaining to the same land office.

BOUNTY-LAND WARRANT RECORDS, 1789-JUNE 30, 1908

The National Archives has U. S. and Virginia bounty-land warrants that were surrendered to the Federal Government for tracts of land in the public domain or for scrip certificates that could be used to purchase tracts of land.[4] The U. S. warrants were issued to certain veterans who served the United States between 1775 and 1855, their heirs, or assignees on the basis of applications approved by the Federal Government.[5] The Virginia warrants were issued by the Commonwealth of Virginia to certain Revolutionary War veterans, their heirs, or assignees on the basis of applications approved by the Commonwealth of Virginia.[6]

These warrants, except for War of 1812 warrants used before 1842, were assignable. Most of the veterans or their heirs sold the warrants on the open market and did not settle on the public domain.

Revolutionary War warrants issued on the basis of legislation dated before 1855 were issued for land in the Virginia Military District of Ohio or the U. S. Military District of Ohio. War of 1812 warrants issued on the basis of acts of Congress dated before 1842 were issued for land in one of three large bounty-land districts: one in Illinois, one in Missouri, and one in Arkansas. The locations of the five Federal bounty-land districts are shown on a map on plate 45 of Charles O. Paullin, Atlas of the Historical Geography of the United States (Washington, 1932). Revolutionary War warrants surrendered in 1830 or later could be exchanged for scrip certificates. Scrip certificates could be used to acquire land elsewhere on the public domain. Warrants surrendered in 1842 or later were not limited to tracts of land in specific areas of the public domain.

The records include records relating to Virginia Revolutionary War warrants surrendered for land in the Virginia Military District of Ohio; records relating to U. S. Revolutionary War warrants surrendered for land in the U. S. Military District of Ohio; records relating to Revolutionary War warrants surrendered for scrip; records relating to U. S. War of 1812 warrants issued for land in bounty-land districts; and records relating to U. S. warrants issued for unspecified land. Each kind of record is described below.

Records Relating to Virginia Revolutionary War Warrants Surrendered for Land in the Virginia Military District of Ohio

Virginia Revolutionary War warrants surrendered for land in the Virginia Military District of Ohio were warrants issued on the basis of service in the Continental Line of Virginia. Originally, the warrants were issued

[4]For information about bounty-land warrants, see "Land Grants for Military and Naval Services" in Payson Jackson Treat, The National Land System, 1785-1820, p. 230-262 (New York, 1910).

[5]The U. S. bounty-land warrant application records are described above in the chapter on "Records of Veterans Benefits."

[6]For information about Virginia bounty-land warrant application records, address the Virginia State Library, Richmond, Va.

for land on the south side of the Green River in Kentucky.[7] But as the result of an agreement between Virginia and the United States, Virginia agreed to cede its western lands to the United States; and Congress, by an act approved June 9, 1794 (1 Stat. 394), provided in effect that holders of Virginia Continental Line warrants could surrender their warrants for tracts of land in a specific area in the Northwest Territory. This area, between the Scioto and Little Miami Rivers, became known as the Virginia Military District of Ohio. Unused Virginia warrants (both for Continental and Virginia State service) could in 1830 or later be exchanged for scrip as described below under "Records Relating to Revolutionary War Warrants Surrendered for Scrip."

The records include entry papers and a map of the Virginia Military District of Ohio. They are described below.

Entry Papers

The records.--The entry papers are dated chiefly 1795-1830. A file includes such documents as a surrendered warrant, a certificate of location, a survey, a power of attorney, an assignment, and an affidavit concerning the heirs of the veteran. The jacket of each file gives the volume and page number of the record copy of the patent in the Bureau of Land Management, Washington 25, D. C. The files are arranged in the order of the numbers of the volumes and the pages.

Indexes to the records.--The indexes identify warrantees and patentees. The index to the names of the veterans of the Virginia Continental Line in whose behalf warrants were issued is in one volume entitled "Virginia Military Warrants, Continental Line, Alphabetical Index to Warrantees (vol. 30)." Entries are alphabetical according to the first letter of the surname. Each entry shows the number of the warrant, the number of acres awarded, the name of the veteran (and heir or assignee, if any), his rank and record of service, and the date on which the warrant was issued.

The names of warrantees have been copied on 3" x 5" cards, which have been interfiled in a consolidated bounty-land warrant card index. The names have also been copied in Gaius Marcus Brumbaugh, Revolutionary War Records, Volume 1, Virginia, p. 387-523 (Washington, 1936).

Some of the warrants were used to obtain land in Kentucky or were converted into scrip. Information about the disposition of a numbered warrant is obtained by consulting the "Abstract of Virginia Military Land Warrants of the Continental Line," in four volumes. In addition to the warrant number there usually appears the name of the veteran, the number of acres of the warrant, and information on the disposition of the warrant. If the land was patented in the Virginia Military District of Ohio, an entry shows also the name of the person for whom the tract was patented and the volume and page number of the recorded copy of the patent. This number indicates the location of the entry file.

The index to the names of patentees is in one volume entitled "Virginia Military Land Patent Index (vol. 34)." Entries are arranged alphabetically according to the first letter of the surname. An entry shows the name of

[7] For information about the Virginia Revolutionary War warrants used to patent land in Kentucky, 1782-93, consult Willard Rouse Jillson, Old Kentucky Entries and Deeds (Louisville, 1926), p. 313-392.

the patentee; the name, rank, and period of service of the warrantee; the number of the warrant; the number of acres patented; and the volume and page number of the recorded copy of the patent. This number indicates the location of the entry file.

Information in the records.--A file shows such information as the name of the warrantee; the name of the patentee; the location of the land in terms of lot, quarter section, township, and range; and the date of the patent. Some files show the dates and places of death of the warrantees, the names of their heirs, and the places of their residence.

Map of the Virginia Military District of Ohio

The records.--A large-scale map, consisting of 25 sheets, showing part of the Virginia Military District of Ohio is available.

Information in the records.--The map shows the name of each patentee, the location of his tract, and the number of acres in it.

Records Relating to U. S. Revolutionary War Warrants Surrendered for Land in the U. S. Military District of Ohio

Under an ordinance of July 9, 1788 (Journals of the Continental Congress, vol. 34, p. 307-308), and an act of Congress of March 3, 1803 (2 Stat. 236), as extended April 15, 1806 (2 Stat. 378), the first U. S. Revolutionary War warrants were issued. Under an act of June 1, 1796 (1 Stat. 490), as amended, the U. S. Military District of Ohio was reserved for holders of these warrants. For information about Revolutionary War warrants exchanged for scrip in 1830 or later and Revolutionary War warrants issued for unspecified land under an 1855 act, see later discussions in this chapter under "Records Relating to Revolutionary War Warrants Surrendered for Scrip" and "Records Relating to U. S. Warrants Issued for Unspecified Land."

The records include warrants and related papers; a register of Army land warrants, 1799-1805; and a record of patentees. Each kind is described below.

Warrants and Related Papers

The records.--The warrants and related papers are dated chiefly 1789-1833. In most instances the surrendered warrant is the only document filed. In some instances an affidavit, power of attorney, or similar document is filed with the warrant.

The warrants and related papers are arranged in two numerical series. The first series, based on the 1788 ordinance, comprises warrants numbered 1-14220, of which most warrants numbered 1-6912 and some with later numbers are missing. The second series, based upon the act of 1803, as extended in 1806, comprises warrants numbered 1-1942.

Index to the records.--The large bounty-land record cards interfiled with the Revolutionary War pension application files and described earlier in the chapter on "Records of Veterans' Benefits" under "Bounty-Land Warrant Application Records" serve as keys to the warrants in the first series. Some of the bounty-land warrant application files interfiled in the same series give the number of the warrant and the number of acres awarded (but not the number "55"); the names and file numbers on these files serve as keys to the warrants in the second series.

Information in the records.--A warrant shows the name of the veteran, the date of issuance of the warrant, and, in appropriate instances, the name of the heir or assignee. Warrants in the second series show the location of the tracts in terms of lot, subdivision, township, and range. Occasional related papers show such information as the names of heirs, their relationship to the veteran, and the places of their residence.

Register of Army Land Warrants

The records.--The register of Army land warrants, 1799-1805, is in one folio-size volume. Entries are arranged chronologically.

Index to the records.--The "Index to the Warrants Register (vol. 218)" contains entries arranged alphabetically to the first letter of the surname of the warrantee or veteran. In addition to the name of the warrantee an entry shows the warrant number, the number of acres shown on the warrant, and the page of the register. The names have been copied on 3" x 5" cards, which have been interfiled in a consolidated bounty-land warrant index.

Information in the Records.--Each entry shows the name of the patentee, the name of the warrantee with his rank, the page and volume number of the recorded copy of the patent in the Bureau of Land Management, and a description of the tract in terms of lot, quarter section, township, and range.

Record of Patentees

The records.--The record of patentees in the U. S. Military District of Ohio is a single index volume. It is entitled "U. S. Military Patents, Ohio Index, vol. 1 (vol. 67)." It serves as an index to the record copies in the four volumes of patents (numbered 1-4, renumbered 210-213) in the Bureau of Land Management. Entries are arranged according to the first letter of the surname in separate listings for each of the four volumes of patents.

Information in the records.--Each entry shows the name of the patentee, the name of the warrantee with his rank, the volume and page citation for the record copy of the patent in the Bureau of Land Management, Washington 25, D. C., and a description of the tract in terms of lot, quarter section, township, and range.

Records Relating to Revolutionary War Warrants Surrendered for Scrip

By 1830 some of the Revolutionary War bounty-land warrants had not been used to patent land. These warrants were of three types: Virginia warrants for land in Kentucky issued on the basis of service in the Virginia State Line; Virginia warrants for land either in Kentucky or the Virginia Military District of Ohio issued on the basis of Virginia Continental Line service; and U. S. warrants for land in the U. S. Military District of Ohio.

By five acts beginning May 30, 1830 (4 Stat. 422), Congress provided that holders of unused Virginia and U. S. Revolutionary War warrants could surrender them for scrip certificates. Scrip certificates differed from warrants in that their use was not limited to a geographical area within the public domain.

A scrip application file includes such documents as the surrendered bounty-land warrant, a power of attorney, an assignment, an affidavit of relationship, and related correspondence.

The records are as follows: records relating to U. S. warrants surrendered 1830-81; records relating to Virginia warrants surrendered 1830-47; and records relating to Virginia warrants surrendered 1852-97. Each kind of record is described below.

Records Relating to U. S. Warrants Surrendered 1830-81

The records.--The records relating to U. S. warrants surrendered 1830-81 are based upon an act of Congress approved May 30, 1830 (4 Stat. 422), as amended 1832-35. They are arranged numerically by application numbers 1-1994 and include records relating to Virginia warrants, 1830-33, which are interfiled in the same numerical sequence.

Indexes to the records.--The name of each veteran listed on a U. S. warrant surrendered for scrip, with the related file number, is entered in the volume "Alphabetical Index to Scrip Claims (vol. 35)." Entries are arranged alphabetically to the first letter of the surname of the veteran. These names have been transcribed on 3" x 5" cards, which have been interfiled in a consolidated bounty-land warrant index.

Information in the records.--Each file shows the name of the veteran, the names of the heirs and their relationship to the veteran, the places of their residences, and the date of the surrender of the warrant.

Records Relating to Virginia Warrants Surrendered 1830-47

The records.--The records relating to Virginia warrants surrendered 1830-47 are based upon an act approved May 30, 1830 (4 Stat. 422), as amended 1832-35. They are arranged in three series. Applications made 1830-33 are interfiled with the files relating to United States warrants, described above. Applications made chiefly 1833-35, numbered 1-225, and applications made 1835-47, numbered 1-970, are in separate series.

Indexes to the records.--The name of each veteran listed on a Virginia warrant surrendered for scrip in 1847 or before, with the related application number, is entered in the volume "Alphabetical Index to Scrip Claims (vol. 35)." Entries are arranged alphabetically to the first letter of the surname of the veteran. These names have been transcribed on 3" x 5" cards, which have been interfiled in a consolidated bounty-land warrant index.

Information in the records.--Each file shows the name of the veteran, the names of the heirs and their relationship to the veteran, the places of their residences, and the date of the surrender of the warrant.

Research aid.--A few of the warrants issued to the veterans named in Gaius Marcus Brumbaugh, Revolutionary War Records, Volume 1, Virginia, p. 323-525 (Washington, 1936), were exchanged for scrip.

Records Relating to Virginia Warrants Surrendered 1852-97

The records.--The records relating to Virginia warrants surrendered 1852-97 are based upon an act of Congress approved August 31, 1852 (10 Stat. 143). They are arranged in individual files numbered 1-1689.

Index to the records.--The name of each veteran listed on a Virginia warrant surrendered for scrip 1852 or later, with the related application number, is indexed in "A List of Claims Satisfied by the Issuance of Scrip, Virginia Military Warrants Act of Aug. 31, 1852 (vol. 43)." Entries are arranged alphabetically to the first letter of the surname of the veteran.

Information in the records.--Each file shows the name of the veteran, the names of the heirs and their relationship to the veteran, the places of their residences, and the date of the surrender of the warrant.

Research aid.--A few of the warrants issued to veterans named in Gaius Marcus Brumbaugh, *Revolutionary War Records, Volume 1, Virginia*, p. 323-525 (Washington, 1936), were exchanged for scrip.

Records Relating to U. S. War of 1812 Warrants Issued for Land in Bounty-Land Districts

As the result of an act of Congress approved May 6, 1812 (2 Stat. 729), and other War of 1812 acts, a noncommissioned officer or soldier who served in the Regular Army for the duration of the War of 1812 was entitled to bounty land in one of three bounty-land districts. These districts, containing 6,000,000 acres in all, were eventually located in Arkansas, Illinois, and Missouri in accordance with the above-mentioned act, as modified by acts of Congress approved April 16 and 29, 1816 (3 Stat. 287, 332).

Until the passage of an act approved July 27, 1842 (5 Stat. 497), the warrants could not be used for land outside these districts and were not assignable.

Each soldier was entitled to 160 acres, except for a few soldiers who were entitled to 320 acres or double bounty in accordance with section 4 of an act of Congress approved December 10, 1814 (3 Stat. 147).

The records.--The records are folded in individual files. Each file includes such documents as the notification of the filing of the warrant with the General Land Office, a power of attorney, and a letter of transmittal. The files are numerically arranged in two series, depending upon the number of acres involved.

Indexes to the records.--A card index is on 3" x 5" cards. Interfiled with the card index are cards relating to War of 1812 soldiers whose surnames begin with A and B and who received benefits under the act of 1850 mentioned below under "Records Relating to U. S. Warrants Issued for Unspecified Land."

Of equal value as an index are the alphabetically arranged post-Revolutionary War series of bounty-land warrant application records described above in the chapter on "Records of Veterans' Benefits." The name of the veteran, the year 1812, the number of acres awarded, and the number of the warrant are needed to locate a desired land-entry file. Such information in abbreviated form appears on each jacket of a bounty-land warrant application file.

Information in the records.--A file contains such information as the name of the veteran; the location of the land in terms of lot, quarter section, township and range; the date of the patent; and the volume and page number of the recorded copy of the patent in the Bureau of Land Management, Washington 25, D. C.

Research aid. --An unindexed volume containing names of soldiers who patented land in the Illinois Bounty Land District, 1817-19, is General Land Office, Lands in Illinois to Soldiers of Late War (26th Cong., 1st sess., H. Doc., 262; serial 369).

Records Relating to U. S. Warrants Issued for Unspecified Land

Beginning in 1847 Congress passed a series of acts which greatly increased bounty-land benefits. The basic acts were dated February 11, 1847 (9 Stat. 125), September 28, 1850 (9 Stat. 520), March 22, 1852 (10 Stat. 4), and March 3, 1855 (10 Stat. 701). They provided for bounty land or additional bounty land for veterans who served in the Revolutionary War or who served between 1790 and 1855, chiefly in the War of 1812, the Indian wars, and the Mexican War; and for heirs of such veterans. As a result veterans and some other persons, such as wagonmasters, who served 14 days during wartime were entitled to bounty land. The acts differ from the previous acts in that the warrants were granted as a reward for service rather than as an inducement to serve. Nearly all these warrants were sold on the market for what they would bring, and the purchasers used them as payment or part payment for tracts of land.

The records. --The files are dated chiefly 1847-55. A file contains such documents as a surrendered bounty-land warrant or a certificate that a bounty-land warrant would be filed in the General Land Office, a power of attorney, an assignment, and an affidavit required of a preemption claimant who had bought the warrant. The files are arranged by year of basic act, thereunder by number of acres awarded, (usually 40, 80, 120, or 160 acres), and thereunder by number of warrant.

Index to the records. --The alphabetically arranged series of bounty-land warrant application records described in the chapter on "Records of Veterans' Benefits" serve as keys to the warrantees named in these files. If a warrant was surrendered on the basis of an application made under one of these acts, the symbols in the file numbers of the related bounty-land warrant application file indicate enough information to locate an entry file. The names of the patentees are not indexed.

Information in the records. --Most files contain no information of genealogical interest about the warrantee as most warrants were sold shortly after they were acquired. In the infrequent cases where the warrantee died possessing the warrant, the file contains the names and places of residence of the warrantee's heirs.

The files identify the patentees by name. They show where the tract acquired by the warrant was located and when it was acquired. In the numerous instances where a patentee purchased a warrant to be applied against a tract in which he had a preemption claim, the file shows when the patentee settled on the land, the size of his household, and the nature of the improvements on the land.

PRIVATE LAND CLAIMS RECORDS, 1789-JUNE 30, 1908

Private land claims are claims to land made on the basis of grants or settlements that took place before the United States acquired sovereignty over the land.[8] These claims relate to persons who claimed to have grants from foreign sovereigns, to descendants of such persons, to pioneers from the United States who settled in these lands with the permission of the foreign governments, and to U. S. citizens who bought up rights to lands acquired under foreign sovereignty and presented them to Federal agencies for the purpose of acquiring title. Much land in what is now the United States was granted or settled between 1685 and 1853 while under the rule of France, Great Britain, Mexico, or Spain. This land was normally described according to the indiscriminate system of land surveying in terms of metes and bounds, and it was normally confirmed in terms of metes and bounds rather than in terms of subdivision, township, and range.

Shortly after the United States acquired land from a foreign government, it established a board of commissioners or other agency to adjudicate private land claims. The agencies that were originally established rarely completed their work; and the uncompleted work was referred to other Federal agencies, such as the district land offices, the U. S. district courts, the Court of Claims, the Supreme Court, the General Land Office, and (for lands deeded by Mexico) the Court of Private Land Claims.

The number and nature of the documents relating to each claim vary greatly. The claim file may include copies and translations of original grants, depositions, affidavits, testimony of witnesses, and a copy of a decision of a court.

Genealogical information in records relating to private land claims varies from the bare mention of the name of the claimant and the location of the land to such additional information about the claimant as his place of residence at the time the claim was made and the names of relatives, both living and dead.

The records described below are not all the records relating to private land claims or even all the records in the National Archives relating to private land claims. They do contain information about most of the claims presented and often give clues as to the location of related documents filed elsewhere. In some instances records, as identified below, of two different Federal agencies contain essentially the same information about the same claim.

The records of private land claims in the National Archives relate to land in parts of the following States: Alabama, Arizona, Arkansas, California, Colorado, Florida, Illinois, Indiana, Iowa, Louisiana, Michigan, Mississippi, Missouri, New Mexico, and Wisconsin.

Each of these States was originally in one of the following areas: the Northwest Territory (Illinois, Indiana, Michigan, and Wisconsin); the

---

[8] The term "private land claim" is sometimes used to apply to land claimed on the basis of circumstances other than those given above. For example, French emigrants claimed land at Gallipolis, Ohio, on the basis of a special act of Congress. Although such claims are not described separately, they are occasionally included or referred to among the records here described.

Mississippi Territory (Alabama and Mississippi); the Louisiana Purchase (Louisiana and the following States of the Missouri Territory: Arkansas, Iowa, and Missouri); the Florida Cession (Florida); and the area in and adjoining the southwest ceded by Mexico (Arizona, California, Colorado, and New Mexico).

The records relating to these areas are described separately below for the Northwest Territory; the Mississippi Territory; Louisiana; the Missouri Territory; Florida; California; and Arizona, Colorado, and New Mexico.

Claims Relating to the Northwest Territory

The Northwest Territory was created in 1787 out of land ceded by France to Great Britain under the Treaty of Paris of 1763 and in turn ceded by Great Britain to the United States under the Treaty of Paris of 1783. The inhabitants, chiefly French, numbered an estimated 2,000 at the time of the establishment of the Territory, residing principally at Vincennes (Ind.), Kaskaskia (Ill.), and Detroit.

By a resolution on August 29, 1788 (Journals of the Continental Congress, vol. 34, p. 472), the Congress of the Confederation provided for claims to land at Vincennes on or before 1783. Pursuant to an act of the Congress of the United States approved March 26, 1804 (2 Stat. 278), a board of commissioners was established to adjudicate land in the portion of the Northwest Territory that became Indiana Territory. Private land claims were presented for lands in what later became the States of Illinois, Indiana, Michigan, and Wisconsin.

Records in the National Archives relating to land claims in the Northwest Territory include records of the boards of commissioners; reports to Congress on private land claims; claims papers of the General Land Office; and records of confirmed private land claims in Illinois. Each type of record is described below.

Records of the Boards of Commissioners

The records.--The records of the boards of commissioners to adjudicate claims in Illinois, Indiana, Michigan, and Wisconsin form a number of small series. Most of the information they contain is duplicated and indexed in American State Papers as described below.

Reports to Congress on Private Land Claims

The records.--The reports to Congress on private land claims are among the records of the U. S. Senate and the U. S. House of Representatives. They are filed by Congress, thereunder by name of committee by which the report was filed, and thereunder chronologically.

Use of the records.--These reports are difficult to use unless they can be identified by committee and date or unless they have been transcribed and indexed in the volumes described below.

Research aids.--Records relating to individual claims presented before boards of commissioners or other Federal agencies between 1790 and 1837 were reported to Congress and transcribed and indexed in U. S. Congress, American State Papers, Class 8, Public Lands (1st Cong.-24th Cong., July 31, 1789-February 28, 1837; Washington, Gales and Seaton, 1832-61). Claims presented 1790 1809 are in volume 1; 1809-15 in volume 2; 1815-24 in volume 3; 1823-27 in volume 4; 1827-29 in volume 5; 1828-34 in volume 6; 1834-35 in volume 7; and 1835-37 in volume 8. Each volume is indexed by name of claimant. Most of these reports, published by Gales and Seaton, were also published in the less complete editions of American State Papers by Duff Green. The reports relating to the Northwest Territory are interspersed among reports relating to private land claims for other geographical areas and among reports relating to other land matters.

Records relating to individual claims between 1826 and 1876 were presented before the two congressional Committees on Private Land Claims and transcribed and published in U. S. Congress, Reports of the Committees on Private Land Claims of the Senate and House of Representatives (45th Cong., 3d sess., S. Misc. Doc. 81; serial 1836, in 2 vols.) Each volume is indexed by name of claimant or subject. There are many unindexed names.

Claims Papers of the General Land Office

The records.--The claims papers of the General Land Office for the Northwest Territory relate only to the States of Illinois, Indiana, Michigan, and Wisconsin.

The papers relating to each claim are filed in separate dossiers. Each dossier contains such documents as correspondence, affidavits, copies of court decisions, and plates with descriptions.

The documents in a dossier range in number from one to many dozens. Documents in many of the dossiers refer to other documents containing earlier information about the claim.

The dossiers form part of a large series of dossiers that are arranged alphabetically by name of State or State group and thereunder numerically by docket number. The dossiers for Illinois, Indiana, and Michigan-Wisconsin are arranged numerically by docket numbers 1-763, 1-542, and 1-960, respectively.

Index to the records.--The National Archives has a photostat of the 85-page index headed "Indiana, Michigan, Ohio, and Wisconsin," which serves in part as an index to the Michigan-Wisconsin files. The Bureau of Land Management, Washington 25, D. C., has retained the indexes for Illinois and Indiana.

Records of Confirmed Private Land Claims in Illinois

The records.--The records of confirmed private land claims in Illinois are in one indexed volume. It is entitled "Abstract of Patent Certificates for Private Land Claims in Illinois." Each entry gives the date of the patent and the location of the land and gives a reference to volume 2 of the edition of American State Papers by Duff Green. Entries are arranged by certificate numbers 1-797 (with some gaps).

Claims Relating to Mississippi Territory

Mississippi Territory was created in 1798, and by 1812 it was enlarged to include the area covered by the present States of Alabama and Mississippi. The area had been occupied by France and Great Britain before the occupation by Spain. Spain renounced its claim to the land above 31° latitude by treaty in 1795, and Congress assumed control over the land below 31° by resolution in 1811. Land settlements date as early as 1763, and land grants date as early as 1715.

A separate board of commissioners adjudicated land claims for each of the following districts: the district west of Pearl River; the district east of Pearl River north of 31°; and the district east of Pearl River south of 31°. Two boards were established by an act of Congress approved March 3, 1803 (2 Stat. 229), and the third by an act approved April 25, 1812 (2 Stat. 713).

The private land claims in the National Archives relating to Mississippi Territory include records of the board of commissioners for the district west of Pearl River; records of the board of commissioners for the district east of Pearl River (north of 31°); records of the board of commissioners for the district east of Pearl River (south of 31°); translations of early records, 1715-1812; reports to Congress of private land claims; and claims papers of the General Land Office. Each kind of record is described below.

Records of the Board of Commissioners for the District West of Pearl River

The records of the board of commissioners for the district west of Pearl River relate to a large portion of the present State of Mississippi. They include claims files; record copies of evidence submitted; record copies of confirmation of claims; certificates of survey of confirmed claims; and journals. Each kind of record is described below.

Claims Files

The records. --The claims files, 1803-5, are arranged numerically 1-2098. Each file is usually a single document consisting of a brief statement of the claim and a map showing its location.

Index to the records. --A one-volume "Index of Claims" has entries arranged alphabetically to the first letter of the surname of the claimant. Following each name is a register number which corresponds to the claims number.

Record Copies of Documents Used as Evidence

The records. --The record copies of documents used as evidence are in eight volumes, A-H, each of which is labeled "Written Evidence Private Grants." They consist largely of copies of original grants in English or Spanish.

Index to the records. --The one-volume "Index of Claims," as stated above, cites after each name a register number. This number is a key to the numerically arranged entries in the one-volume "Register of Claims Presented." Entries in this register cite in appropriate instances the volumes and page numbers for copies of the documents used as evidence.

Record Copies of Certificates of Confirmation

The records. --The record copies of certificates of confirmation of claims are in four volumes. Entries are arranged according to type of certificate, A, B, or C, and thereunder by number, except that entries for letter C, in volume 4, are out of order.

Index to the records. An "Index to Confirmation Certificates" is in one volume.

Certificates of Survey of Confirmed Claims

The records.--The certificates of survey of confirmed claims are unbound. They are arranged according to type of certificate, A, B, or C, and thereunder by number.

Index to the records.--The "Index to Confirmation Certificates" serves also as an index to certificates of survey.

Journals

The records.--The journals, with entries chiefly 1803-7, are in five volumes. Entries record chronologically the action taken on each claim. The pages are numbered consecutively in one sequence, 1-1811. A sixth volume in the series is a register of claims.

Index to the records.--The "Index of Claims," described earlier, cites the page or pages of the journal relating to each claim.

Records of the Board of Commissioners for the District East of Pearl River (North of 31°)

The records.--The records of the board of commissioners for the district east of Pearl River (north of 31°) relate to portions of Alabama and Mississippi. They include two volumes of proceedings, 1804-5.

Index to the records.--An indexed docket book contains page references to the two volumes.

Records of the Board of Commissioners for the District East of Pearl River (South of 31°)

The records.--The records of the board of commissioners for the district east of Pearl River (south of 31°) relate to very small portions of Alabama and Mississippi. They include an unindexed volume labeled "Reports, Land Office, Jackson (Court House), Mississippi." This volume contains summary information about many early claims.

Translations of Early Land Records

The records.--The translations of early land records are translations into the remaining two languages of documents, 1715-1812, that were originally written in English, French, or Spanish. They are in one unindexed volume and concern the area that became Alabama. They were compiled at St. Stephens, Ala., from records of the land office in 1841 pursuant to an act of the Alabama legislature.

Reports to Congress on Private Land Claims

The records.--The reports to Congress on private land claims relating to the Mississippi Territory are of the types described above under "Claims Relating to the Northwest Territory," where reference is made to American State Papers.

Claims Papers of the General Land Office

The records.--The claims papers of the General Land Office for Alabama and Mississippi are arranged numerically by docket numbers 1-593 and 1-544, respectively. They are of the types described above under "Claims Relating to the Northwest Territory."

Indexes to the records.--The National Archives has a photostat of a 19-page index to the Mississippi claims papers. The Bureau of Land Management, Washington 25, D. C., has retained the index to the Alabama claims papers.

Claims Relating to Louisiana

The State of Louisiana was created in 1812 chiefly from Orleans Territory. This Territory embraced an area originally settled by France, acquired by Spain in 1762, retroceded to France in 1800, and purchased by the United States in 1803 as a part of the Louisiana Purchase. The remaining part of the State of Louisiana, an area east of the Mississippi River that had once formed a part of British West Florida, became a part of the United States by resolution of Congress in 1811.

Of three early boards of commissioners one was for the eastern district of Orleans Territory, one for the western district of Orleans Territory, and one for the area between the Mississippi and Pearl Rivers (north of Lake Pontchartrain) that had been a portion of British West Florida. The first two boards were created pursuant to an act of Congress approved March 2, 1805 (2 Stat. 327). The third was established by an act of Congress approved April 25, 1812 (2 Stat. 713).

The materials in the National Archives relating to private land claims in Louisiana include records of the board of commissioners for the eastern district of Orleans Territory; nonrecord transcripts of records of the board of commissioners for the western district of Orleans Territory; nonrecord transcripts of records of the board of commissioners for the district east of the Mississippi River and west of the Pearl River; nonrecord transcripts of records relating chiefly to Natchitoches and Monroe (Ouachita) claims; reports to Congress of private land claims; and claims papers of the General Land Office. Each kind of material is described below.

Records of the Board of Commissioners for the Eastern District of Orleans Territory

The records.--The records of the board of commissioners, established at New Orleans, for the eastern district of Orleans Territory include the decisions of the board, in four volumes.

Index to the records.--There is a one-volume index to the records volumes, giving names of claimants.

Nonrecord Transcripts of the Records of the Board of Commissioners for the Western District of Orleans Territory

The records.--The nonrecord transcripts of the records of the board of commissioners, established at Opelousas, for the western district of Orleans Territory were copied from the records at the new State Capitol Building, Baton Rouge, La. They were typed and indexed by the Survey of

Federal Archives in Louisiana under the Work Projects Administration and are in two binders.

Nonrecord Transcripts of the Records of the Board of Commissioners for the District East of the Mississippi River and West of the Pearl River

The records.--The nonrecord transcripts of the records of the board of commissioners, established at Greensburg, for the district east of the Mississippi River and west of the Pearl River (north of Lake Pontchartrain) were copied from records at the new State Capitol Building, Baton Rouge, La. They were typed and indexed by the Survey of Federal Archives in Louisiana under the Work Projects Administration, 1939-42, and are in nine binders. Eight of them concern land claims notices; a ninth concerns British grants, 1768-79.

Nonrecord Transcripts Relating Chiefly to Natchitoches and Monroe (Ouachita) Claims

The records.--The nonrecord transcripts relating to Natchitoches and Monroe (Ouachita) claims are in an indexed binder labeled "Land Claims and Other Documents." They were copied from records at the new State Capitol Building, Baton Rouge, La., by the Survey of Federal Archives in Louisiana under the Work Projects Administration. They relate to Laffite and Rio Hondo claims; Natchitoches claims and reports; Indian claims and reports; and Monroe and Ouachita claims.

Reports to Congress on Private Land Claims

The records.--The reports to Congress on private land claims relating to Louisiana are of the types described above under "Claims Relating to the Northwest Territory," where reference is made to American State Papers.

Claims Papers of the General Land Office

The records.--The claims papers of the General Land Office for Louisiana are arranged numerically by docket numbers 1-5323. They are of the type described above under "Claims Relating to the Northwest Territory."

Index to the records.--The National Archives has a photostat of a 145-page index to the names of claimants.

Claims Relating to Missouri Territory

Missouri Territory comprised that part of the Louisiana Purchase north of Orleans Territory. The area had originally been settled by the French, but for most of the period after 1762 it was governed by the Spanish. Private claims were made for land in the area that became the present States of Arkansas, Iowa, and Missouri.

The records in the National Archives relating to private land claims in Arkansas, Iowa, and Missouri include claims papers of the General Land Office relating to Arkansas, Iowa, and Missouri; reports to Congress on private land claims for the Missouri Territory; and records of confirmed land claims in the State of Missouri. Each kind of record is described below.

Claims Papers of the General Land Office Relating to Arkansas, Iowa, and Missouri

The records.--The claims papers of the General Land Office relating to Arkansas, Iowa, and Missouri are arranged numerically by docket numbers 1-227 (with one unnumbered), 1-2, and 1-2046, respectively. They are of the type described above under "Claims Relating to the Northwest Territory."

Indexes to the records.--The Bureau of Land Management, Washington 25, D. C., has retained the indexes to each series.

Reports to Congress on Private Land Claims for the Missouri Territory

The records.--The reports to Congress on private land claims for the Missouri Territory are of the type described above under "Claims Relating to the Northwest Territory," where reference is made to American State Papers.

Records of Confirmed Land Claims in the State of Missouri

The records.--The records of confirmed land claims in the State of Missouri are in a folio-size volume, 1803-62. The volume contains the following exhibits: A. Claims confirmed by the old or first board of commissioners in Missouri; B. Town and village lots; C. Extensions of grants over the quantity confirmed by the first board; D. Concessions; E. Settlement right; F. New Madrid claims; G. Hunt's list; H. Claims recommended and confirmed by an act of Congress 4th July, 1836, with exceptions; I. Grants of land by the Governor General of Louisiana; K. Confirmation by the Supreme Court of the United States; L. Confirmations by special acts of Congress; and M. Valid but not finally confirmed claims. An entry shows such information as the date, the name of the confirmee, the name of the original claimant, the grant of land claimed, and references. A master index gives the names of confirmees.

Claims Relating to Florida

The land occupied by the State of Florida was formerly owned, at different times, by Spain and Great Britain. Under terms of the treaty of 1819, Spain agreed to cede Florida to the United States. On May 8, 1822 (3 Stat. 709), a board of commissioners was established to adjudicate private land claims. On March 3, 1823 (3 Stat. 754), the work of the board was confined to West Florida, and an additional board was established for East Florida.

The records in the National Archives relating to private land claims in Florida include transcripts of the proceedings of the boards of commissioners; claims papers of the General Land Office; records of confirmed private land claims; and reports to Congress on private land claims. Each kind of record is described below.

Transcripts of the Proceedings of the Boards of Commissioners

The records.--The transcripts of the proceedings of the boards of commissioners are mimeographed briefed translations of the records, which were deposited with the Florida Department of Agriculture, Tallahassee, Fla. They are identified as follows: Historical Records Survey, Florida, Spanish Land Grants in Florida; Briefed Translations from the Archives of the Boards of Commissioners for Ascertaining Claims and Titles to Land in the Territory of Florida . . . Prepared by the Historical Records Survey, Division of Professional and Service Projects, Work Projects Administration (Tallahassee, State Library Board, 1940-41, 5 indexed vols.). Volume 1 concerns unconfirmed claims; volumes 2-5 concern confirmed claims.

Claims Papers of the General Land Office

The records.--The claims papers of the General Land Office for Florida are arranged numerically by docket numbers 1-506. They are of the type described above under "Claims Relating to the Northwest Territory."

Index to the records.--The index has been retained by the Bureau of Land Management, Washington 25, D. C.

Records of Confirmed Private Land Claims

The records.--The records of confirmed private land claims are in four indexed volumes dated 1857-80. They are entitled "Record and Condensed History of Private Land Claims in the State of Florida Showing the Connective Lines of Each Claim with the Public Surveys." The volumes contain plats of the individual claims and give descriptions of them in terms of metes and bounds.

Index to the records.--A photostat of a 23-page master index of claimants is available. The spellings of some of the names vary from those in indexes in the individual volumes.

Reports to Congress on Private Land Claims

The records.--The reports to Congress on Florida private land claims are of the type described above under "Claims Relating to the Northwest Territory," where reference is made to American State Papers.

Claims Relating to California

Spain granted lands in California as early as 1769, and Mexico granted lands there when it took possession. Between 1822 and 1846 many claimants filed claims before Mexican authorities in support of claims based on Spanish or Mexican grants. The area came into possession of the United States by the treaty of Guadalupe Hidalgo in 1848, and by 1852 Congress established a board of commissioners to adjudicate private land claims in the State of California. The decisions of this board could be appealed to the courts.

Records in the National Archives relating to private land claims in California include Expedientes and other records of claims presented to the Mexican Government, 1822-46; bound records of the California board of commissioners, 1852-56; a record copy of a map identifying private land grants, 1944; claims papers of the General Land Office; and reports to Congress on private land claims. Each kind of record is described below.

Expedientes and Other Records of Claims Presented to the Mexican Government

The records.--The expedientes and other records of claims presented to the Mexican Government are dated 1822-46. They are usually in Spanish and document individual claims based on Spanish or Mexican grants. They were used by the California board of commissioners to adjudicate claims. Most of them are unbound and filed in two numerical series, one for complete expedientes and the other for incomplete expedientes.

Index to the records.--A printed index shows by name of claimant the date, location, and number of each complete or incomplete expediente. It is entitled "Catalogue of the Original Expedientes" in General Land Office, Annual Report of the Commissioner of the General Land Office for the Fiscal Year Ending June 30, 1880, p. 455-495 (Washington, 1881). Entries in the index are arranged to the first letter of the surname.

Use of the records.--Most of these records were translated and transcribed in the bound records of the California board of commissioners (described below), which are easier to consult than the original records.

Bound Records of the California Board of Commissioners

The records.--The bound records of the California board of commissioners are dated 1852-56. They were created in conformity with an act of Congress approved March 3, 1851 (9 Stat. 631). They include petition books; journals; records of evidence with depositions of witnesses; copies of English and Spanish documents, with translations of Spanish documents; atlases; and decisions. The entries are usually arranged chronologically within each series of volumes.

Index to the records.--A volume labeled "California Index to Private Land Claims" (vol. 5) lists in one alphabetical sequence the names of localities, the names of original claimants, and the names of "present" claimants. It serves as a key to volume 4, labeled "Index," which identifies the 813 claims by docket number. Under each numbered entry are citations to documents in the various series of bound volumes.

Research aid.--See General Land Office, Report of the Commissioner of the General Land Office for the Fiscal Year Ending June 30, 1880, p. 395-454 (Washington, 1881), which lists by docket number the names of 813 claimants, with the corresponding localities, the names of original claimants, and the numbers of the expedientes, if any.

Related records.--Transcripts of the proceedings of the California board of commissioners were made pursuant to an act of Congress approved August 31, 1852 (10 Stat. 99). The National Archives has the set that was sent to the Attorney General of the United States. The transcripts are unbound and those for each claim are filed together by docket number. They are convenient to consult because the copies of documents relating to an individual claim are in a single dossier, but they are not complete and the handwriting is not always easy to decipher.

Record Copy of a Map Identifying Private Land Grants, 1944

The records.--A record copy of a map identifying private land grants in California was prepared by the General Land Office in 1944. It is entitled "State of California, Compiled from the Official Records of the

General Land Office and Other Sources," and is on a scale of 12 miles per inch. Each of the 553 confirmed claims is numbered on the map, which contains both a numerical and an alphabetical list of claims or localities.

Index to the map.--A photostat of a 56-page typed index to the plat books in the National Archives shows the name of claimant for each confirmed claim and the name of the claim. The map number of the claim can be derived from the alphabetical list of the claims on the map. Since it is difficult to locate the number on the map without knowing the name of the county in which the grant was located, the reader may need to see General Land Office, Annual Report of the Commissioner of the General Land Office for the Fiscal Year Ending June 30, 1881, p. 533-549 (Washington, 1881). For each claim this list shows alphabetically by name of claim the land commissioner number, the map number, the name of the confirmee, the date when the land was patented or related information, the name of the county in which it was located, and the total area.

Claims Papers of the General Land Office

The records.--The claims papers of the General Land Office for California are filed numerically by docket numbers 1-620. They are of the type described above under "Claims Relating to the Northwest Territory."

Index to the records.--The National Archives has a 52-page typed index that shows the names of claimants.

Reports to Congress on Private Land Claims

The records.--The reports to Congress on private land claims for California are of the type described above under "Claims Relating to the Northwest Territory." California claims were of too late a date to be reported in American State Papers.

Claims Relating to Arizona, Colorado, and New Mexico

Spain had granted land as early as 1685 in the area that became Arizona, Colorado, and New Mexico. Later Mexico granted land there. In 1848 and 1853 the area was ceded by Mexico to the United States. On July 22, 1854 (10 Stat. 308), the office of Surveyor General for New Mexico was created, and the Surveyor General was authorized to report on claims in New Mexico.

The records in the National Archives relating to private land claims in Arizona, Colorado, and New Mexico include partial reports of the Surveyor General of New Mexico; claims papers of the General Land Office for Arizona and Colorado-New Mexico; and reports to Congress on private land claims. Each kind of record is described below.

Reports of the Surveyor General of New Mexico

The records.--The partial reports of the Surveyor General of New Mexico cover only the years 1856-59; volume 1 has claims 1-16 and volume 2 has claims 17-38.

Index to the records.--A volume labeled "Old Index of Private Land Claims in New Mexico, Arizona, and Colorado" contains references to 193 claims including the above-mentioned 38 claims.

Research aid.--Volume 1 of Department of the Interior, Report of the Secretary of the Interior for the Fiscal Year Ending June 30, 1885 (Washington, 1885), contains, on pages 535-552, a list of colonial documents relating to grants of land by the Spanish and Mexican governments in the archives of the office of the Surveyor General of New Mexico. This list shows the "archive" number and the year of the document, the name of the original claimant or other person, the nature of the document, and the name of the county in which the land claimed is located. The entries are arranged alphabetically to the first letter of the surname.

Claims Papers of the General Land Office

The records.--The claims papers of the General Land Office for Arizona and Colorado-New Mexico are arranged numerically by docket numbers 3-19 and 1-215 respectively. They are of the type described above under "Claims Relating to the Northwest Territory."

Indexes to the records.--There are two separate typed indexes, one for Arizona and one for Colorado New Mexico.

Reports to Congress on Private Land Claims

The records.--The reports to Congress on private land claims for Arizona, Colorado, and New Mexico are of the type described above under "Claims Relating to the Northwest Territory." Private land claims for these States, however, were not reported in American State Papers.

Use of the records.--It is often difficult to ascertain information about the land owners or settlers on the land before the United States took possession. This is because most of the name indexes give only the names of persons who presented their claims to U. S. Government agencies. Some of the indexed publications identify the earlier persons.

THE NUMERICAL SERIES, JULY 1, 1908-DECEMBER 31, 1950

The records.--The numerical series consists of land-entry files on the basis of which patents were issued between July 1, 1908, and December 31, 1950. These files consist of cash, homestead, and all other types of entries completed within this period. They are arranged in numerical sequence.

Index to the records.--The Bureau of Land Management, Washington 25, D. C., has retained a 3" x 5" card index which lists the names of the patentees with the numbers of the corresponding land-entry files.

Information in the records.--Each file shows the name of the patentee; the place of his residence; the description of the tract in terms of subdivision, section, township, and range; the date of the patent; and the number of the file, which is also the number of the record copy of the patent in the Bureau of Land Management, Washington 25, D. C. Additional information in the file depends upon the type of land entry as described previously in this chapter.

Related records.--Files relating to land entries that have been canceled, relinquished, or rejected during this period have been retained in part by the Federal Records Center, Alexandria, Va., and in part by the Bureau of Land Management.

GENERAL OBSERVATIONS

Use of the Land-Entry Records

The genealogical use of land-entry papers is complex. The requirements for a search vary, depending upon the nature of the facts available. If a person received a patent to land after June 30, 1908, a searcher for his record should see the index described under "The Numerical Series," above. If a person was entitled to a patent between 1800 and June 30, 1908, on the basis of purchase or condition of settlement, and the land was located in Alabama, Arizona, Florida, Louisiana, Nevada, Utah, or Alaska, a searcher should see a 3" x 5" card index in the National Archives. If a person received a patent to land in Ohio through a district land office, 1800-1820, a searcher should see the book index relating to that land office in the Bureau of Land Management, Washington 25, D. C. If a person received a patent to land in the Virginia Military District of Ohio or the U. S. Military District of Ohio, a searcher should see the indexes described above pertaining to those respective districts under "Bounty-Land Warrant Records."

If a person received a patent to land and a description of the land in terms of subdivision, section, township, and range is known, the related land-entry file can be ascertained through the use of the tract books in the Bureau of Land Management, Washington 25, D. C. If a description of the tract is unknown, it is often possible to ascertain the description through a deed in the county where the tract is located.

A searcher might ascertain the township and range number by consulting an atlas and the population census schedules described in the chapter on "Population and Mortality Census Schedules;" and he might ascertain the location of the tract by consulting, in the Bureau of Land Management, the entries in the tract books covering the township concerned.

If the approximate date of the patent and an approximate location of the land are known, one can search the chronologically arranged entries in an abstract book in the National Archives for the appropriate land office. The National Archives has an index which helps to identify the land office having responsibility for a given area at a given time. It is entitled "Index List of Offices" and is in four volumes.

Record Groups

The land-entry records are in Record Group 49, Records of the Bureau of Land Management, except the unbound transcripts of the proceedings of the California Board of Land Commissioners, which are in Record Group 60, General Records of the Department of Justice, and the reports to Congress, which are in Record Group 46, Records of the United States Senate, and Record Group 233, Records of the United States House of Representatives.

VIII. OTHER RECORDS OF GENEALOGICAL VALUE

RECORDS CONCERNING INDIANS

The National Archives has many records concerning Indians, chiefly the Indians who maintained their tribal status. They are dated primarily 1830-1940.

The records include lists relating to Indian removal; annuity pay rolls; annual census rolls; special rolls relating to the Eastern Cherokees; claims relating to the Eastern Cherokees; estate files; and Carlisle Indian School files. These records are described below.

In addition, the National Archives has population census schedules and bounty-land warrant application files which in part relate to Indians. The population census schedules, described in the chapter on "Population and Mortality Census Schedules," include the names of Indians who had severed their tribal affiliations, but normally there is no way to identify Indians as such before 1870. The bounty-land warrant application files relating to service later than the Revolutionary War, described in the chapter on "Records of Veterans' Benefits," include a segregated alphabetical file relating to tribal Indians with the name of each Indian, his military organization, and the dates of his service appearing on the related jacket.

Many records in Federal custody relating to the Five Civilized Tribes in Oklahoma are in the Federal Records Center, Fort Worth, Tex.

Lists Relating to Indian Removal

The records.--The lists relating to Indian removal concern chiefly the migration of Cherokees, Chickasaws, Choctaws, Creeks, and Seminoles, both before and after their removal to the western lands. Some of these lists are census lists of the tribe made prior to their emigration, while others are muster rolls of the emigrating parties of Indians. They are dated primarily 1830-52. The muster rolls are arranged chronologically by the date of emigration and are, for the most part, not indexed. The census rolls are arranged by the town or district in which the Indian lived and are indexed.

Information in the records.--The records vary in content. Some show only the names of the heads of families. Others show in addition the number of persons in each family by age group and sex, and for some tribes that have moved westward, the original place of residence of each head of family.

Annuity Payrolls

The records.--The annuity payrolls resulted from treaties or acts of Congress providing that the Federal Government make annual payments to tribal members for a stated period of time. They are usually in bound volumes, which are arranged by name of tribe and thereunder chronologically. Those in the National Archives are dated 1848-1940 but are of most use genealogically for the period before the beginning of the annual census rolls in 1885.

Information in the records.--As a minimum the records show the name of each head of family or more usually the name, age, sex, amount per capita payment, and signature or mark of each member.

Annual Census Rolls

The records.--The annual census rolls were created pursuant to an act approved July 4, 1884 (23 Stat. 98). Those in the National Archives are dated 1885-1940. They are arranged alphabetically by name of Indian agency, thereunder by name of tribe, and thereunder by year. The names of the individual Indians on the earlier rolls are not arranged alphabetically, but by about 1916 most of the agencies were submitting their yearly census lists with the individual names arranged alphabetically. No census rolls were submitted for the Five Civilized Tribes of Oklahoma or for the Eastern Cherokees before 1898.

Information in the records.--The rolls usually show for each Indian the Indian or English name or sometimes both, sex, relationship to the head of family and sometimes to another Indian named on the roll, and age; some of the earlier rolls are less complete. A name is often assigned to two numbers on a roll, one being the order in which the name appears on the roll and the other the order in which the name appears on the previous roll. The earlier rolls often show the names of persons who were born or died during the year and their dates of birth or death; after 1924 such information was recorded on separate interfiled rolls.

Special Rolls Relating to the Eastern Cherokees

The records.--The special rolls relating to the Eastern Cherokees were prepared to reimburse individual members for land and for other purposes. They are dated 1835-36, 1848-49, 1851-52, 1868-69, 1884, 1907-8, 1909-10, and 1924. Entries on the rolls are alphabetized or indexed. For further details, see Gaston Litton, "Enrollment Records of the Eastern Band of Cherokee Indians," in North Carolina Historical Review, 17:199-231 (July 1940).

Information in the records.--All the rolls give the name of each head of family. Nearly all give the name and age of each member of the tribe. Some indicate relationships to other enrolled members.

Claims Relating to the Eastern Cherokees

The records.--The claims in the case of the Eastern Cherokees vs the United States (general jurisdiction case No. 23214) were filed before the U. S. Court of Claims pursuant to a provision of an act of July 1, 1902 (32 Stat. 726).

Information in the records.--An individual claim file often contains such information as the full English name and Indian name of the claimant, residence, and date and place of birth; the name and age of each brother and sister; the name and place of birth of each grandparent and the name, residence, and, where appropriate, the date of death of each child; and sometimes identification of ancestors of a claimant with persons living when some of the early rolls were made. There is a two-volume alphabetical index to these claims files.

Estate Files

The records.--The estate files consist of wills, reports on heirship, and related papers. Those in the National Archives are dated 1910-40, with some as early as 1907. They form a part of a general classification file and are arranged by jurisdiction, thereunder by file number, and thereunder by date.

Indexes to the records.--Card indexes are in the Bureau of Indian Affairs.

Information in the files.--The files usually show for each decedent his name, tribe, place of residence, date of death, and age at date of death. If a report on heirship is filed, it normally shows additional information such as the name of spouse and the date of marriage of heir and spouse, the names and dates of marriage of their parents, the names of their brothers and sisters, and the names of their children.

Carlisle Indian School Files

The records.--The files of the Carlisle Indian School, Carlisle, Pa., include 5" by 8" record cards, which are alphabetized, and individual student folders. The records are dated 1879-1918.

Index to the records.--A card index to the individual student folders is available.

Information in the records.--Each record card relates to an individual student and shows his English name, Indian name, agency, nation, band, home address, degree of Indian blood, age, and the dates of his arrival and discharge. Each folder relates to an individual student and includes the name of one of his parents and his school record.

RECORD GROUPS

The records concerning Indians are in Record Group 75, Records of the Bureau of Indian Affairs, except that some of the special rolls relating to Eastern Cherokees and all the claims relating to Eastern Cherokees are in Record Group 123, Records of the United States Court of Claims.

CIVILIAN PERSONNEL RECORDS

The records.--The National Archives has many records relating to civilian personnel in the executive and judicial branches of the Federal Government. Most of them are dated from the time of the establishment of an agency to about 1910.

The types of records vary from agency to agency, from position to position, and from date to date. They include letters of application, letters of recommendation or endorsement, letters of acceptance, registers of appointment, oaths of office, surety bonds for bonded officials, and letters of resignation or other evidences of termination of service.

The arrangement of these records is usually quite complex. Surety bonds, other than those relating to postmasters, are filed together. Record cards for bonds dated 1789-1910 and for those dated 1911-15 are arranged alphabetically by name of bonded official. Most records relating to employment with an agency, however, are filed with other records relating to the same agency. They are often arranged by type of record, thereunder chronologically, and are generally not indexed. Letters, such as letters of application and letters of recommendation, are sometimes interfiled among large correspondence files which may be inadequately indexed. A few agencies, however, filed letters of application with letters of recommendation, and sometimes other personnel records, in separate name files. Following is a list giving the names of the executive departments that maintained extensive segregated name files of letters of application and recommendation, the types of personnel concerned, the inclusive dates covered by the records for each type, and a statement concerning the arrangement of the records:

State Department, appointees under the jurisdiction of the Department plus others, especially in the earlier years those under the War and Treasury Departments, 1797-1901[1]	By Presidential administration, thereunder alphabetical by personal name
Treasury Department, bureau heads and other headquarters staff, ca. 1835-1909	Alphabetical by personal name
Treasury Department, field staff, ca. 1835-1909	By name of bureau or title of position (such as Bureau of Internal Revenue or Collector of Customs), thereunder by name of State, thereunder by number of district or name of city, thereunder alphabetical by personal name
War Department, all employees, 1861-87	By calendar year, thereunder alphabetical by personal name
Justice Department, field staff, 1853-1933	Before 1901, by Presidential administration, thereunder by name of State or Territory, thereunder alphabetical by personal name; beginning in 1901, by name of State or Territory, thereunder by office, and thereunder alphabetical by personal name

[1]Applications and recommendations for office during the Presidency of George Washington are in the Manuscript Division of the Library of Congress.

Interior Department, Presidential appointees, 1849-1907	By Presidential administration, thereunder by name of bureau, thereunder by place, thereunder by personal name; indexed
Interior Department, others, 1879-1906	By calendar year, thereunder numerically; indexed

The application and recommendation files in the departments also include a number of smaller series, among them some relating to unsuccessful applicants for positions.

The Federal Records Center, 111 Winnebago Street, St. Louis 18, Mo., maintains most extant personnel folders for separated Federal employees. Most of the earliest folders begin about 1910, but some begin earlier.

Information in the records.--Most records relating to a civilian employee show his full name, the position he held, the name of the agency, and the place and terminal dates of his employment. Some show in addition the State, Territory, or country of the employee's birth; his age; the place from which he was appointed; and his compensation.

Letters of application and letters of recommendation may include considerable biographical data such as the name of a relative of the applicant and his relationship to the applicant, the nature of the applicant's previous employment, his political affiliation, and his political activity. The material in a file varies considerably and sometimes is voluminous if the position sought is an important one.

Use of the records.--In requesting a record, a searcher should provide the full name of the employee, the name of the agency where he was employed or sought employment, and the place and approximate date of his employment.

Record groups.--Personnel records are in many record groups, often in the record group set up for the general records of the executive department concerned.

RECORDS OF THE REVENUE-CUTTER SERVICE

The records.--The National Archives has service records for the officers and crews of the Revenue-Cutter Service, 1791-1915, and for the officers of its successor, the U. S. Coast Guard, 1915-29. The records dated before 1833 are fragmentary and relate almost entirely to officers.

The records relating to officers consist of record books of officer personnel, registers of commissions, applications for appointments and commissions as officers or cadets, with related correspondence, and officer personnel records. The record books of officer personnel, 1797-1919, which are individually indexed, contain, by name of officer, citations to the location of pertinent correspondence in various series of correspondence files. The registers of commissions, 1791-1909, are individually indexed by name of officer. Files of applications for appointments and commissions as officers or cadets, ca. 1833-90, are arranged alphabetically by name of applicant. The officer personnel records, chiefly 1890-1929, which include records of former Revenue-Cutter Service officers whose term of service extended beyond 1915, are in alphabetically arranged folders.

The records relating to crew members of the Revenue-Cutter Service include "muster rolls and pay rolls" (after 1871 muster rolls) and shipping articles. These series of rolls are unbound monthly reports, dated 1832-1914. They are arranged by name of vessel and thereunder chronologically and are not indexed. The shipping articles are in bound volumes dated 1863-1915, those for each vessel in a single unindexed volume.

Information in the records.--The records relating to officers usually show the names of the States from which appointed, dates of birth, and, for those who died in the service, the dates of death; they often show biographical information about careers before the officers entered the service, and sometimes the names of their relatives, their successive dates of appointment, the posts they held, and the nature of the duties they performed.

The records relating to crew members vary somewhat in content depending largely upon the purpose of the record. A "muster roll and pay roll" shows the name, and, when appropriate, the mark, of each crew member. A muster roll shows for each crew member the name; rating; date and place of enlistment; city, town, or county and State of birth; age; occupation; personal description; number of days served during the reported month; whether he was detached, transferred, or discharged, had deserted, or had died; and if so, when and where. The shipping articles show for each crew member the name; rating; wages per month; date and place of enlistment; city, town, or county and State of birth; age; occupation; and personal description. They also contain his signature or mark. Some shipping articles dated 1907 and later show names and addresses of the "nearest" relative or beneficiary.

Record group.--The records are in Record Group 26, Records of the United States Coast Guard.

CLAIMS RECORDS

The records.--The National Archives has many types of claims records in addition to the pension and bounty-land warrant application records and the Cherokee Indian claims records described in the chapter on "Records of Veterans' Benefits" and the first section of this chapter, respectively. The claims records are in a large number of series which are identified under the names of the agencies or other administrative bodies before which the claims were presented. The papers relating to an individual claim are often in a single folder or jacket and consist of a filled-out form, correspondence, and supporting documents.

The claims records include records relating to private claims brought before the U. S. Senate and the U. S. House of Representatives, French spoliation claims resulting from the quasi-war with France at the close of the 18th century, claims resulting from the Civil War, and patents for inventions.

Information in the records.--The records relating to an individual claim vary considerably in the information that they contain. They normally show the name of the claimant, his age, and the place of his residence at the date of filing; and they sometimes contain the names of parents, grandparents, or other family members and other personal information. A patent application, however, rarely contains more personal information than the name and address of the applicant.

Indexes to the records.--Many series of claims records are arranged numerically but are accompanied by indexes to the names of the claimants. A few of these indexes that may be of special use to the genealogist are mentioned below.

Lists of private claims brought before the Senate and the House of Representatives were printed as Congressional documents. Each list is arranged alphabetically by name of claimant and shows the nature or object of the claim, the Congress and session before which it was brought, and the nature and number or date of the report. The following tabulation shows the coverage of each list and the citation to the Congressional document.

Senate, 14th to 46th Congresses (1815-81), S. Misc. Doc. 14, 46th Cong., 3d sess. (serials 1945-1946)
Senate, 47th to 51st Congresses (1881-91), S. Misc. Doc. 266, 53d Cong., 2d sess. (serial 3175)
House, 1st to 31st Congresses (1789-1851), H. Misc. Doc. (unnumbered), 32d Cong., 1st sess. (serials 653-655)
House, 32d to 41st Congresses (1851-71), H. Misc. Doc. 109, 42d Cong., 3d sess. (serial 1574)
House, 42d to 46th Congresses (1871-81), H. Misc. Doc. 53, 47th Cong., 1st sess. (serial 2036)
House, 47th to 51st Congresses (1881-91), H. Misc. Doc. 213, 53d Cong., 2d sess. (serial 3268)

Indexes to other claims records are listed below:

U. S. Court of Claims. French Spoliation Awards by the Court of Claims of the United States Under the Act of January 20, 1885 (Washington, 1934). Gives the name of each original claimant who suffered loss as the result of French depredations on American vessels, 1793-1801, and whose heirs were compensated on the basis of claims filed in 1885 or later. Arranged alphabetically by name of original claimant.

"Index to Claimants: French Spoliation Claims, Department of Justice, Court of Claims Section." An unpublished volume among the records of the Court of Claims Section, listing the claims alphabetically by name of heir, administrator, or other representative of the original claimant.

U. S. Commissioners of Claims. Consolidated Index of Claims Reported by the Commissioners of Claims to the House of Representatives From 1871 to 1880 (Washington, 1892). Gives the name of each claimant before the commission usually known as the Southern Claims Commission for "stores or supplies taken or furnished during the rebellion for the use of the army of the United States in States proclaimed as in insurrection against the United States," his State of residence, the claim number, and the action on each claim. Arranged alphabetically by name of claimant.

An unpublished index among the records of the Quartermaster General to claims submitted to the Quartermaster General, primarily under an act of July 4, 1864, by loyal citizens in States that were not in insurrection. Arranged alphabetically by name of claimant.

U. S. Patent Office. List of Patents for Inventions and Designs, Issued by the United States From 1790 to 1847 (Washington, 1847). Gives

747-596 O - 64 - 10

the subject of each invention or discovery, the name of the patentee, his place of residence, and the date the patent was issued. Arranged by class, with an index by name of person. Annual lists of patents issued after 1847 were published in the Annual Reports of the Commissioner of Patents.

Record groups.--The claims records are in many record groups. Private claims brought before the Senate are in Record Group 46, Records of the United States Senate; those brought before the House of Representatives are in Record Group 233, Records of the United States House of Representatives; French spoliation claims are in Record Group 123, Records of the United States Court of Claims, and Record Group 205, Records of the Court of Claims Section (Justice); claims resulting from the Civil War that were brought before the Southern Claims Commission are in Record Group 217, Records of the United States General Accounting Office, and Record Group 233, Records of the United States House of Representatives: similar claims brought before the Quartermaster General are in Record Group 92, Records of the Office of the Quartermaster General; and patents for inventions are in Record Group 241, Records of the Patent Office.

PASSPORT APPLICATIONS

The records.--The National Archives has passport applications received by the Department of State, with related records, 1791-1905.

Passports were not required of United States citizens traveling abroad until World War I except for a short time during the Civil War. They were frequently obtained when not required, however, because of the added protection they might afford.

A passport application was originally a letter, later a filled-out form. An application was often accompanied by such supporting papers as an obsolete passport, a copy of a birth record, a certificate of citizenship, or a letter of transmittal. Since 1861 an oath of allegiance has been part of or has accompanied the application.

The main series of passport applications, 1830-1905, is in bound volumes. The registers or indexes to these applications date from 1834 and vary as follows:

Dates	Indexes or registers
1834-59	Overlapping book registers, usually alphabetized to first letter of surname
1860-79 (and 1850-52)	Master 3" by 5" card index
1880	3" by 5" card index
1881-1905	Book indexes

Another series, the series of emergency passport applications, is also in bound volumes, 1877-1905. These applications for passports or renewals of passports were made at foreign service posts abroad. They are arranged by name of post and thereunder chronologically. Related book registers are alphabetized to the first letter of the surname.

Other series include a register of passports issued, 1810-17; bound record copies of passports issued, 1817-34; and a register of passports issued to persons destined for Santo Domingo Island, 1799-1801.

In addition to the records just described, there are passport records in the National Archives that were maintained by the diplomatic and consular posts abroad. Those before 1874 were not always duplicated in the Department's own files. For the most part they are scattered and contain relatively little information. They include a volume from the American Legation in Great Britain entitled "Passport letters," 1795-1812, and a related register.

Information in the records.--A passport application varies in content, the information being ordinarily less detailed before the Civil War period than afterward. It usually contains the name, signature, place of residence, age, and personal description of the applicant; the names or number of persons in his family intending to travel with him; the date; and, where appropriate, the date and court of naturalization. It sometimes contains the exact date and place of birth of the applicant and of his wife and minor children accompanying him, if any; and, if the applicant was a naturalized citizen, the date and port of his arrival in the United States and the name of the vessel on which he arrived.

Use of the records.--The use of these records is restricted. Persons wishing to confirm age or citizenship from these records that are less than 75 years old should write to the Passport Office, Department of State, Washington 25, D. C.

Record groups.--These records are in Record Group 59, General Records of the Department of State, or in Record Group 84, Records of the Foreign Service Posts of the Department of State.

RECORDS CONCERNING THE DEATHS OF AMERICANS ABROAD

The records.--The National Archives has death notices relating to many Americans residing or traveling in foreign countries, chiefly 1857-1922, with some as early as 1792. They were made in conformity with an act approved April 14, 1792 (1 Stat. 255).

The death notices are in the form of reports called "despatches" from American consular and sometimes diplomatic officials abroad. They are interfiled with despatches dealing with many other subjects and are in many different series. For the period 1857-1922, however, there is a series of bound and usually indexed volumes containing death notices that have been abstracted from the despatches. Some include newspaper clippings.

Information in the records.--A death notice normally shows the name of the decedent, the place of his former residence in the United States, the date and place of his death, and the name and the post of the official who reported the death. If the notice is in a despatch, it sometimes contains an inventory of the estate of the deceased and brief identifying information. If the notice is in the series of bound volumes and dated 1871 or later, it normally contains the number and date of the despatch to which it relates.

Use of the records.--The despatches before 1857 cannot be used effectively unless the year and place of death are known.

Record group.--These records are in Record Group 59, General Records of the Department of State.

RECORDS CONCERNING MERCHANT SEAMEN

The National Archives has lists of American seamen impressed by Great Britain before the War of 1812 or imprisoned during the war, 1793-1815; many applications for seamen's protection certificates and related materials, 1796-1866 and 1916-40; crew lists for vessels entering and clearing some Atlantic and Gulf of Mexico ports, 1803-1919; and shipping articles for vessels entering and clearing many ports, 1840-1938. Each kind of record is described below.

Lists of American Seamen Impressed

The records.--The unbound lists of American seamen impressed by Great Britain before the War of 1812 or imprisoned during it, 1793-1815, are arranged chronologically and are unindexed. The bound lists, in three volumes, are for 1793-1802 only. The latter are indexed to the first letter of the surname.

Information in the records.--Each entry shows the name of the seaman and such related information as the date of his capture, the date of his application for release, the name of the vessel from which he was taken, the name of the vessel on which he was impressed or the name of the place of his imprisonment, and occasionally the number of his seaman's protection certificate and the name of the port from which it was issued.

Applications for Seamen's Protection Certificates

The applications for seamen's protection certificates, 1796-1866, were made under an act approved May 28, 1796 (1 Stat. 477). On the basis of the application an American seaman was issued a protection certificate which was used for identification, initially in connection with possible impressment by Great Britain.

The records.--The National Archives has applications for the port of Philadelphia, but they are unindexed. In addition it has bound and unbound abstracts for most ports. The bound abstracts, 1808-16, are in one volume, which is indexed to the first letter of the surname. The unbound abstracts, 1815-66, are arranged by name of port and are indexed on two series of 3" by 5" cards. One series relates to New York City, the other to most other ports. The applications for seamen's protection certificates, 1916-40, are arranged by name of port and usually thereunder chronologically. Those for the ports of Boston, New York, and Philadelphia are indexed.

Among the records of the New York Customhouse are a few certificates of citizenship that may originally have been filed with the applications. They were made by local authorities, are dated chiefly 1797-1850, and are arranged by name of State and thereunder alphabetically by personal name.

Information in the records.--An application for a seaman's protection certificate shows the name of the seaman, his age, often the place of his birth, his personal description, his signature or mark, and, if he was naturalized, the date of naturalization and the name of the court that granted it. Beginning in 1916, it shows the date of the seaman's birth instead of his age and contains his photograph.

Crew Lists

In compliance with an act of February 28, 1803 (2 Stat. 203), "for the further protection of American seamen," crew lists were required to be filed with collectors of customs by masters of American vessels departing from and arriving at United States ports.

The records.--The National Archives has crew lists for New York, 1803-1919, New Orleans, 1803-1902, Philadelphia, 1803-99, and for some other ports, usually for parts of the 19th century.

Information in the records.--Crew lists show the name, place of birth and residence, and a description of each member of the crew.

Research aids.--Vessel arrival and clearance registers are present for many ports, but not necessarily for the entire period covered by the crew lists of a given port. These registers may assist the searcher in ascertaining the date of arrival or departure of a ship.

Some of the information on the New Orleans lists in the period 1803-25 has been abstracted in 15 typed volumes. Data given include the name of the seaman, his rank, State or country of birth, and nationality. Each of these 15 volumes is indexed by the name of the seaman, name of the master, and name of the ship in a composite alphabetical index.

Shipping Articles

Shipping articles were required by an act approved July 20, 1790 (1 Stat. 131), but they were not regularly filed with collectors of customs until the passage of act of July 20, 1840 (5 Stat. 394). Under an act of June 7, 1872 (17 Stat. 262), shipping commissioners were appointed in certain ports to superintend the shipping and discharge of seamen, and they largely took over this function of the collectors of customs.

The records.--There are shipping articles for many ports, usually for 1840-1938 or some part of that period. They are arranged by port and thereunder basically chronologically, though with some variations. Shipping articles for New York and some other ports are indexed.

Information in the records.--Shipping articles show for each seaman his name (including his signature or mark), the State or country of his birth, his age, and a personal description.

RECORD GROUPS

The lists of American seamen impressed are in Record Group 59, General Records of the Department of State, as are the bound abstracts, 1808-16, of applications for seamen's protection certificates; the unbound abstracts, 1815-66, are in Record Group 36, Records of the Bureau of Customs, and the applications for seamen's protection certificates, 1916-40, are in Record Group 41, Records of the Bureau of Marine Inspection and Navigation; and crew lists are in Record Group 36. In general, shipping articles up until 1872 are in Record Group 36 and ones after that year are in Record Group 41, but the dividing date varies from port to port.

RECORDS OF NATURALIZATIONS OUTSIDE THE DISTRICT OF COLUMBIA

The first naturalization act passed by Congress on March 26, 1790 (1 Stat. 103), provided that an alien who desired to become a citizen should apply to "any common law court of record, in any one of the states wherein he shall have resided for the term of one year at least." Under this and later laws aliens were naturalized in Federal courts and also in State and local courts.

Records of naturalization proceedings in Federal courts are usually in records of the district court for the district in which the proceedings took place. These court records may still be in the custody of the court, they may have been transferred to a Federal Records Center operated by the General Services Administration, or they may have been transferred to the National Archives. Naturalization proceedings are often recorded in the minutes of both district and circuit courts; for example, see the minutes of both courts for the Southern District of New York, 1789-1913, now in the National Archives. Also in the National Archives, among the records of the U. S. District Court for the Eastern District of Virginia, are a few declarations, petitions, and certificates of naturalization for the years 1855 and 1867-96. And among the records of the U. S. District Court for the Western District of Virginia at Abingdon are a few petitions for naturalization, 1910-17, and a few petitions to set aside certificates of naturalization, 1909. Other naturalization records do not appear to have been transferred to the National Archives with court records.

Records of naturalization proceedings in State or local courts would normally be in the custody of the clerk of the court. Publications of the Historical Records Survey, described near the end of this chapter, are sometimes useful in finding and using State and local court records.

Two Historical Records Survey publications that relate specifically to naturalization records are Index to Naturalization Records, Mississippi Courts, 1798-1906 (prepared by the Old Law Naturalization Records Project, Division of Community Service Programs, WPA, and issued in Jackson, Mar. 1942; classified in the National Archives Library as HRS 1857A), which lists individuals alphabetically under the county in which they were naturalized; and Guide to Naturalization Records in New Jersey (prepared by the New Jersey Historical Records Program, Division of Community Service Programs, WPA, and issued in Newark, 1941; classified in the National Archives Library as HRS 1337), which describes series of naturalization records by county.

If a naturalized citizen or a person who had declared his intention to become a citizen applied for a homestead, or if a naturalized citizen applied for a passport before 1906, the application would normally be in the National Archives and give the name of the court where the naturalization took place. Duplicates of records relating to persons naturalized since September 27, 1906, are deposited with the Commissioner of Immigration and Naturalization, Washington, D. C., and are confidential.

Photocopies of Naturalization Records

To centralize the information in the naturalization records, which are among the records of more than 5,000 Federal, State, and other courts, the

Work Projects Administration in the late 1930's began to make photographic copies of the records and to index them. Some of these copies and indexes are now in the National Archives.

The records.--The records consist of 5" x 8" photocopies of naturalization documents, 1787-1906, filed by courts in Maine, Massachusetts, New Hampshire, and Rhode Island. They are arranged by State, thereunder by court, and thereunder by date of naturalization.

Index to the records.--The index is on 3" x 5" cards arranged by name of petitioner for naturalization. A card contains the name and location of the court and identifies the papers by volume and page number and petition or entry number. The printed cards have spaces, often left blank, for other data that may be in the naturalization papers. The index cards are filed according to the Soundex system; that is, alphabetically by the first letter of the surname, thereunder by the sound of the surname, and thereunder alphabetically by the given name. There are some index cards for New York and Vermont, although neither the related naturalization records nor copies of them are in the National Archives.

Information in the records.--For each naturalization there are usually two pages of forms with spaces for some or all of the following: the petition for citizenship, the oath of allegiance to the United States, affidavits relating to U. S. residence, and a record of citizenship. Other information on the forms usually includes place and date of birth and of arrival in the United States, place of residence at the time of applying for citizenship, and sometimes the name of the ship on which the immigrant arrived and his occupation.

Use of the records.--A searcher may make an abstract of a naturalization record in the National Archives. According to section 346 of an act approved October 14, 1940 (54 Stat. 1163), however, it is a felony for any person "to print, photograph, make, or execute, or in any manner cause to be printed, photographed, made, or executed, without lawful authority, any print or impression in the likeness of any certificate of arrival, declaration of intention, or certificate of naturalization or of citizenship, or any part thereof."

Record group.--The records are in Record Group 85, Records of the Immigration and Naturalization Service.

Civil Service Commission List of Naturalization Certificates

The records.--A volume entitled "List of Naturalization Certificates Sent to the U. S. Attorney for Review, and Returned by Him to the Board of Civil Service Examiners, of Persons Taking Civil Service Examinations, 1905-06," was transferred to the National Archives from the New York district office of the Civil Service Commission. Naturalization certificates for persons taking Federal civil service examinations in New York State are entered under the initial letter of the surname and thereunder chronologically by date the certificate was sent to the U. S. attorney.

Information in the records.--For each naturalization certificate are given the name of the court that issued it, the name of the person who signed it, the kind of civil service examination taken and where, and the date the certificate was returned by the attorney.

Record group.--The volume is part of Record Group 146, Records of the United States Civil Service Commission.

RECORDS CONCERNING INHABITANTS OF THE DISTRICT OF COLUMBIA

The National Archives has certain court records relating to the part of the District of Columbia that was not retroceded to Virginia. They include naturalization records, transcripts of wills, administration papers relating to the estates of decedents, guardianship papers, and indentures of apprenticeship. They form part of the records of the courts created under terms of an act approved February 27, 1801 (2 Stat. 103), and later acts. Each kind of record is described separately below.

Naturalization Records

The records.--The naturalization records, 1802-1926, are based on an act approved April 14, 1802 (2 Stat. 153), and later acts. The ones described here, for the years 1802-1906, are less detailed than those filed in accordance with an act approved June 29, 1906 (34 Stat. 596).

The records include declarations of intention (or certified copies if the declarations had been filed elsewhere), petitions to become citizens (which succeeded "proofs of residence"), and orders of admission to citizenship. A declaration of intention normally preceded a proof of residence or a petition to become a citizen by two or more years, but the declaration was sometimes not required if the citizen had an honorable discharge from certain military service or had entered the country when a minor. The petition to become a citizen and the order of admission were handled at or about the same time and were often recorded on the same page. The early orders of admission to citizenship are normally available only in the minute books.

A list of the basic series of naturalization records to about 1906, with dates of each series, follows: unbound declarations of intention and such related records as proofs of residence, arranged chronologically, 1802-1903; a bound volume of abstracts (and, for 1818, transcripts) of declarations of intention, 1818-65; bound volumes of declarations of intention, 1866-1906; bound volumes labeled "naturalization records" consisting in part of orders of admission, 1824-1906; and a volume index to most series of naturalization records, 1802-1907.

Information in the records.--The declarations of intention normally show for each declarant his name, age, allegiance, the country or exact place of his birth, the date of his declaration, and, for those dated before 1866, the date and place of his arrival and the place of his embarkation. The proofs of residence contain the names of two citizens who testified.

The bound "naturalization records" show, for 1824-39, the date of admission of each person to citizenship and usually the same information as that contained in the declaration of intention and proof of age; for 1839-65, the name of each person and the term and year of admission, arranged by first letter of surname; for 1866-1906, the name, place of birth, and age of the person, the date of his declaration of intention, statement of honorable discharge, or statement of arrival as a minor (at first, before the age of 18, and later, 21); and from 1903, the date of arrival.

Use of the records.--See the statement on "use of the records" on the preceding page.

Transcripts of Wills

The records.--There is in the National Archives a series of transcripts of wills probated in the District of Columbia, 1801-88, which is arranged chronologically in 25 volumes. A second series of transcripts, 1801-1919, and the original wills are deposited with the Register of Wills and Clerk of the Probate Court, U. S. Courthouse, Washington 25, D. C.

Indexes to the records.--The index to the first series of transcripts, 1801-88, a one-volume "General Index to Recorded Wills," gives by name of maker of the will not only the volume and page numbers to that series but also the volume and page numbers for the second series. A two-volume index labeled "Probate Index to Wills Recorded," 1801-1919, gives the volume and page numbers for the second series only.

Information in the records.--A will normally shows the name and place of residence of the maker, the date of the will and its probate, the name of the executor or executors, and often the names of children or of other family members.

Administration Papers Relating to the Estates of Decedents

The records.--The administration records, 1801-78, relate to the estates of decedents. They include bound administration dockets, of which those between 1837 and 1853 are missing, and unbound administration case files.

Index to the records.--A volume entitled "Probate Index" indexes both the dockets and the case files.

Information in the records.--A docket shows the name of the administrator or, if the deceased had made a will, the name of the executor; the name of the decedent and the place he had resided; the names of sureties; and the date letters of administration were granted. A case file usually contains the inventory of the estate, the account or periodical accounts of the administrators or executors, the related vouchers, and sometimes a petition for administration and related correspondence. It normally shows the name of the decedent, the nature and value of his estate, and the amount distributed to each named heir. It sometimes shows the date of decease of the decedent and the names of heirs at law.

Guardian Records

The records.--The guardian records, 1801-78, relate to estates inherited by wards of the court, chiefly minors. They include bound guardian dockets and the unbound case files of guardian papers.

Index to the records.--The only complete index to the names of the wards is the one-volume "Probate Index." It indexes both the dockets and the case files.

Information in the records.--A docket shows the names of the guardian and the sureties; the name of the decedent and the place he had resided; the names of the wards and, if they were minors, usually the dates of their births or their ages; and the value of the estate. A case file normally contains the account or periodical accounts of the guardian, the related vouchers, and often related correspondence. A case file usually shows the name of the guardian and the amounts distributed periodically to each ward.

Indentures of Apprenticeship

The records.--The indentures of apprenticeship, 1801-74, are arranged chronologically. The originals are unbound, but copies, which exist for 1801-11 only, are bound in one volume.

Indexes to the records.--Both the unbound originals and the bound copies are indexed.

Information in the records.--An indenture of apprenticeship is a single document which shows the name and usually the age of the apprentice, the name of one of his parents, the name and trade of his master, and the term of his apprenticeship.

RECORD GROUP

The records are in Record Group 21, Records of District Courts of the United States.

DIRECT TAX LISTS FOR PENNSYLVANIA

The National Archives has direct tax lists for Pennsylvania, made as of October 1, 1798, under the provisions of an act approved July 9, 1798 (1 Stat. 580), for the valuation of lands and dwelling houses and the enumeration of slaves, and an act of July 14, 1798 (1 Stat. 597), to lay and collect the tax on these.

The records.--The records consist mainly of assessment and collection lists, with a few other kinds of lists that were made from these in complying with various aspects of these laws and subsequent ones. Slave lists among the Pennsylvania records are comparatively few. The lists of most use for genealogical research are the Particular Lists A and B. Particular List A relates to dwelling houses with outhouses on lots not exceeding 2 acres and of over $100 in value. Particular List B relates to lands, lots, buildings, and wharves except as described in A. Some of the information in the particular lists was used in compiling other lists, which should be consulted if the particular lists are missing. Most of the lists are in booklets and are arranged by division, thereunder by district, thereunder by county, thereunder by township, and thereunder by type of list. These records have been microfilmed.

Information in the records.--Particular List A shows in general for each dwelling house the name of the occupant; the name of the owner; the location and dimensions of the dwelling house and outhouses; the building materials used; the number of the stories and of windows; and the valuation. Particular List B shows in general for each occupant of lands, lots, buildings, and wharves the name of the occupant, the name of the owner, the number and dimensions of the dwelling house and outhouses, the number and description of all other buildings and wharves, the location and name of adjoining proprietors, the number of acres of land, and the value.

Record group.--The records are in Record Group 58, Records of the Internal Revenue Service.

Location of other tax lists.--The extant direct tax lists for Massachusetts, including Maine, are in the New England Historic Genealogical Society, 9 Ashburton Place, Boston, Mass. The lists for Boston have been transcribed, printed, and indexed in Boston, Registry Department, "The Statistics of the United States' Direct Tax of 1798, as Assessed on Boston" (Boston, 1890), volume 22 of Records Relating to the Early History of Boston. The extant direct tax lists for Maryland and the District of Columbia are in the Maryland Historical Society, 201 West Monument Street, Baltimore, Md. The Georgia Department of Archives and History in Atlanta has lists of owners of slaves in the First and Second Divisions of Burke County, 1798. The location of the other direct tax lists is unknown.

HISTORICAL RECORDS SURVEY PUBLICATIONS

The records.--The National Archives has record copies of most of the publications of the Historical Records Survey, including some of genealogical interest, 1936-43.

This set includes inventories of the archives of many counties in the United States. The proportion of counties in a State for which inventories were completed varies from complete coverage for the counties of North Carolina to no inventories for any of the counties of Connecticut, Maine, and Rhode Island. Only one county inventory was completed for Vermont (Lamoille County) and the National Archives does not have a record copy of this inventory, although it has copies of most of the ones that were prepared. There are also copies of inventories of Federal archives in the States; some copies of inventories of State archives, municipal and town archives, and church archives; church directories; guides to vital statistics records in various States; transcripts of records, including those relating to Spanish land grants in Florida; and other inventories and miscellaneous publications.

The publications of the Historical Records Survey are listed in Work Projects Administration, Bibliography of Research Projects Reports, Check List of Historical Records Survey Publications (Washington, 1943. WPA Technical Series, Research and Records Bibliography No. 7).

The National Archives does not have the microfilm publications and the unpublished project material of the Historical Records Survey. The names and addresses of the State depositories for the unpublished project material appear in an appendix of the bibliography just cited.

Information in the records.--The contents vary depending upon the subject. The inventories of the county archives give a description, with total volume and terminal dates, of many county archives in courthouses and elsewhere. Among such archives are wills, land records, birth and death certificates, marriage licenses, and naturalization records.

Use of the records.--A copy of the bibliography is available in the National Archives. Some large libraries throughout the country have not only the bibliography but also many Historical Records Survey publications.

Record group.--The records are in Record Group 69, Records of the Work Projects Administration.

U. S. GOVERNMENT PRINTING OFFICE : 1964 O - 747-596

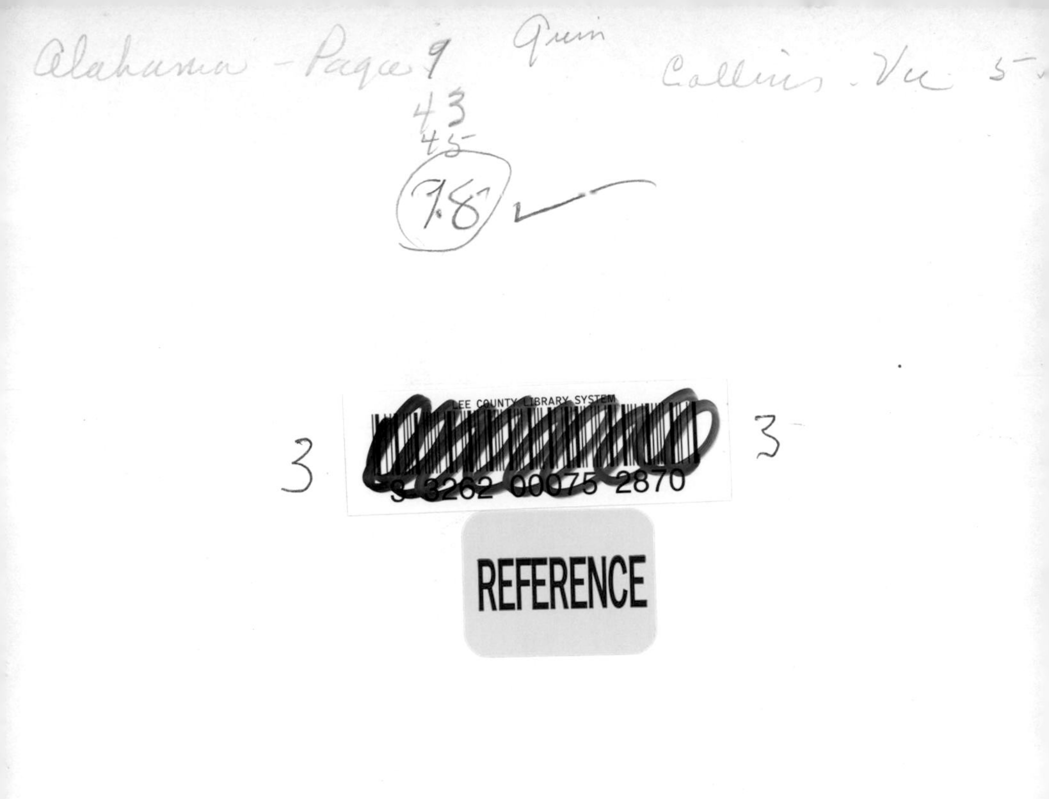
Alabama - Page 9
Quin
Collins - Va 5
43
45
78
3
LEE COUNTY LIBRARY SYSTEM
3 3262 00075 2870
3
REFERENCE